I0091381

Love
Law

What to know before you say `I do!'

By Elizabeth Fairon

The material in this book is provided for information purposes only. The reader should consult with his or her personal legal, financial and other advisors before utilising the information contained in this book. The author and the publisher assume no responsibility for any damages or losses incurred during or as a result of following this information.

There are many legal principles included in this book which the author has explained in her own way. If required, specific references can be provided on request.

All names referred to in this book have been changed to protect the identity of the individual.

INDEPENDENT INK

Published 2023 by Independent Ink
PO Box 1638, Carindale
Queensland 4152 Australia

© Elizabeth Fairon 2023

The moral right of the author has been asserted.

All rights reserved. Except as permitted under the *Australian Copyright Act 1968*, no part of this book may be reproduced or transmitted by any person or entity, in any form or by any means, electronic or mechanical, including photocopying, recording, scanning or by any information storage and retrieval system, without prior permission in writing from the author.

Cover design by Catucci Design
Back cover photography by Jason Malouin
Typeset in 11/17 pt Bembo by Post Pre-press Group, Brisbane

Cataloguing-in-Publication data is available from the National Library of Australia

ISBN 978-0-6458852-2-4 (pbk)
ISBN 978-0-6458852-3-1 (epub)

For Tasha

who asked 'how is that next book coming along'

Contents

Introduction

Starting out on a new relationship can be fun and exciting. There are new experiences every day. You learn how to like each other, to spend time with each other, to love each other, and to live with each other. You learn about each other's habits, the good ones and the bad ones, and ultimately you decide that you would like to live together and perhaps spend the rest of your lives together.

It is an enjoyable, thrilling time in a relationship. Mostly you find yourself living blissfully unaware of what is happening around you. Whether you marry or not, some call this the 'honeymoon period'.

Now this is not a book written to tell you about all the things that can go wrong in a relationship, how divorce and separation works and where to get advice – you'll find that information in my book *Trust Yourself: How Empowered Decision Making Will Help You Resolve Your Family Law Matter.* This book is about making sensible decisions from the start, knowing how the law can impact you and your rights from the outset so that you can get on with enjoying your life and your relationship.

I have had a lot of conversations over the years with clients and friends saying, 'I wish I knew that before.' Or 'If only I knew then what I know now.' And 'Why didn't you tell me that sooner?' It's those conversations that have led me to put together this guide for some key things to think about before you say I do, or yes, let's.

Among these pages, you'll find information about important things to consider at the beginning of any relationship. It does not matter whether you are getting married or committing to a long-term de facto relationship. It does not matter whether you are in a same sex or different-sex relationship. The law treats all relationships equally. You will find information about blending families, managing your property, the importance of having a will and other documents you might consider.

I've found that the more aware you are of information and knowledge as it applies to your circumstances, the more empowered you are to make good decisions.

To be aware means that you are concerned and well informed about a particular situation or development. You are conscious and alert to the importance of your circumstances.

If you can be more aware of particular aspects of life and law as they may apply to you, you can make informed decisions about your future. It's within that context that the concept for this book has evolved and the things you should be **aware** of on your journey into love and law are the following:

A   All types of relationships

W   What about the kids

A   Apples & Oranges (because it sounds more interesting than 'Assets')

R   Ready for the Future

E   Empowered by information

And so in **Part One** you will learn about how the law looks at **relationships** – de facto or marriage, regardless of gender.

In **Part Two** we'll have a look at the **impact of new relationships on children** – you won't find information about whether having children is for you, but a deep dive into relationships where one or both parties already have children.

In **Part Three** you will find information about **how to think about the property you have**, how to protect it if it's significant, and whether you need to consider a financial agreement (prenuptial agreement).

In **Part Four** we'll look to the future and talk about the **importance of wills and enduring powers of attorney** and what happens when you don't have these important documents.

Finally in **Part Five** we'll look at **why getting advice early in your relationship is important**, the type of advice you should get and how information (from the right sources) will empower you to make good relationship decisions.

In the conclusion I pull all of the critical information together for you.

Finally, in the **Resources** section at the end of this book you will find key information and contact details for organisations that can assist you.

Note that this book is written as an information guide only. It should not be read as advice specific for your personal circumstances. You should always consult with a lawyer to obtain legal advice about your individual circumstances. You may need to see a lawyer who can give you advice about family law matters or estate planning. Make sure you consult with a lawyer who practices in the area of law you need advice on.

It is on that basis that I commend this book to you. While it is important that you do get legal advice about your own individual matter, what you will find in this book is information in a format you can understand to equip you to move forward to finding a solution to your legal issue. I hope you find empowerment in reading and learning from it, as much as I have from writing it.

All types of relationships

THE EVOLUTION OF THE RELATIONSHIP

Relationships have always been an essential aspect of human life. From the beginning of civilisation to today, people have been seeking and nurturing relationships with others. However, the nature of relationships has changed significantly over time.

In traditional societies, families usually arranged marriages, and personal choice had little to do with it. Male dominance was prevalent, and women were expected to obey their husbands. The focus of the relationship was on procreation and the survival of the family. Divorce was uncommon and frowned upon.

The industrial revolution changed everything. The migration of people to cities, changes in the economy and the social structure, and the rise of individualism led to new relationships. People started forming relationships based on personal choice and free will. The traditional arranged marriage began to decline, and people started looking for partners who could satisfy their emotional and sexual needs. As education and literacy rates improved, people became exposed to new ideas and lifestyles, and the value of love and emotional satisfaction in relationships started gaining importance.

The 1960s marked another significant shift in relationships. The feminist movement gained momentum, and women started questioning their societal role. The ideals of gender equality, individualism and self-expression became popular. The concept of open relationships and free love emerged, and people started breaking the traditional norms of monogamy, commitment and sexual exclusivity. The advent of the pill and no-fault divorce also changed the landscape of relationships.

With the advent of technology, especially social media, relationships have taken a new turn in recent years. Social media has made forming connections, keeping in touch and maintaining long-distance relationships easier. Online dating websites and apps have allowed people to meet potential partners outside their social circles. The parameters of relationships have become more fluid, and people are experimenting with different types of connections, such as polyamory.

Relationships have come a long way from the traditional forms to modern-day relationships. The shift towards individualism and self-expression has created an environment where people can choose their partners and define their relationships. However, this freedom has come with its own set of challenges. As society evolves, relationships will change, and people will continue experimenting with new connections.

DOES THE LAW MAKE A DISTINCTION FOR SAME-SEX RELATIONSHIPS?

It's important to deal with this very important question straight away. The short answer is no. **There is now no legal distinction between a same-sex couple and a heterosexual couple.**

This wasn't always the case though. Marriage was previously defined as a union between a man and a woman. This changed in 2017 when the definition of marriage changed. Nowadays anyone over a certain age is free to marry whomever they wish. Marriage is now defined as the union of two people to the exclusion of all others, voluntarily entered into for life.

For this reason, this is the only reference you'll see in this book to that historical distinction. We approach the information in this book so that it applies to all types of relationships.

WHEN DOES THE LAW GET INVOLVED?

So you've been dating for a little while now and have taken the plunge to move in together. Your six-month anniversary of cohabiting ticks over. Your friends or associates say, 'Six months – they can take half your property now . . .' Right? No – not quite.

It's a common misconception that if you have lived together with someone for six months, then your relationship status is elevated to a point where one spouse might be able to claim property of their partner. While living together is one factor that is taken into account, the law is a little more complex than that.

De facto relationships at law

A de facto relationship exists under the following circumstances.

A person is in a **de facto relationship** with another person if:

(a) the persons are not legally married to each other and

(b) the persons are not related by family and

(c) having regard to all the circumstances of their relationship, they have a relationship as a couple living together on a genuine domestic basis.

The factors set out in the Family Law Act (section 4AA) that are taken into account when considering whether two persons have been living together as a couple on a **genuine domestic basis** include as follows:

- the duration of the relationship
- the nature and extent of their common residence
- whether a sexual relationship exists
- the degree of financial dependence or interdependence, and any arrangements for financial support, between them
- the ownership, use and acquisition of their property
- the degree of mutual commitment to a shared life
- whether the relationship is or was registered under a prescribed

law of a state or territory as a prescribed kind of relationship

- the care and support of children
- the reputation and public aspects of the relationship.

A party to a de facto relationship can bring an application for property orders or spouse maintenance where the court is satisfied:

(a) that the period, or the total of the periods, of the de facto relationship is at least two years or

(b) that there is a child of the de facto relationship or

(c) that a party to the de facto relationship has made substantial contributions to property of the parties or the welfare of the family and failure to allow the application would result in serious injustice to that party or

(d) that the relationship is or was registered under a prescribed law of a state or territory.

So you can see that **it is not as straight forward as simply living together for two years**. There are a number of factors to keep in mind when determining if a de facto relationship exists. If you are serious about your relationship long-term and you have no plans to marry, you may consider registering your relationship as evidence of the existence of your commitment. A benefit of doing this is to avoid unnecessary distress should you separate. You are less likely to have an argument about whether a relationship existed.

What if one party claims there was no de facto relationship?

Commonly from a separation perspective, a key issue can be whether a de facto relationship exists at law.

Case Study

Suzanne and Felicity lived in an on-again, off-again relationship for over five years. They met and started going out together in about 2012. They lived together for periods at Felicity's parents' home, and they lived separately at other times. They did not have any children. They had a sexual relationship. They presented as a couple to their friends and family. Some years into their relationship, they purchased a property together. They split the mortgage repayments equally. Felicity paid for the rates and utilities. About six months after they purchased this property, Suzanne and Felicity separated their living arrangements. They continued to see each other on and off, and maintained their sexual relationship. About a year after the purchase of the property, Suzanne ended the relationship.

It is more than likely that a de facto relationship exists in these circumstances. Suzanne and Felicity own property together, they presented as a couple to their family and friends, and they lived with each other from time to time.

Whether a relationship exists at all is often argued about in matters with short relationships, particularly where one party to the relationship has significant assets in their own name and the existence of a de facto relationship may mean that another party possibly has a claim to those assets.

If it is difficult to establish on evidence that a relationship existed as set out in the earlier section defining a de facto relationship, the person who is trying to assert a relationship may have little or no option to pursue the matter under the Family Law Act. It can be a costly experience if an application is made to the court and it is unsuccessful. It is best to get some advice about the status of your relationship.

What if you are in a relationship with more than one person?

Case Study

Jasmine was in a long-term relationship with George for nine years. George said the relationship was only for three years. Jasmine had a property in her name at the beginning of the relationship. George also had a property in his name. During the relationship, George acquired two further properties in his own name. Jasmine and George lived together in George's property. They presented to their family and friends as a couple. They attended family gatherings, weddings and funerals as a couple. Jasmine was able to produce invitations addressed to both of them throughout their relationship.

While they didn't have any children, Jasmine and George both made contributions to the relationship. Jasmine managed the accounts and at times paid bills for George on his behalf. Jasmine assisted in finding the properties that George purchased.

Upon separation, George claimed that they did not have a de facto relationship. The basis of this claim was that they had no joint property and that George had been maintaining a relationship with another woman for the last three years. George and this other woman did not live together, though, because she was still married to another man.

Now this is quite a complex matter which all comes down to the evidence that both parties can produce about their relationship. The key point here, however, is that just because George was in a relationship with another person at the same time as his relationship with Jasmine, doesn't mean that the de facto relationship between Jasmine and George didn't exist.

Many cases seeking a property settlement involving a de facto relationship often also seek a declaration that the relationship existed at law, particularly where it is disputed by one party, or ended very close to the two-year period. For that reason, if you are clear at the outset about your relationship and when it started, you are less likely to have difficulties later.

MAKING IT LEGAL

Registering your de facto relationship

You can find information about how to register your de facto relationship by contacting the registry of births, deaths and marriages in your state or territory. This aspect of family law is still managed by the individual states within Australia. **Most states and territories have a mechanism by which you can register a civil partnership.** It is sometimes called a civil partnership and otherwise called a registered or recognised relationship. In Queensland, it is called a civil partnership; Victoria notes the registration as a domestic relationship. The Northern Territory and Western Australia are the two jurisdictions in Australia that do not offer the registration of relationships or official domestic partnership schemes. If you live in either of these states or territories, you should contact a lawyer for some advice about how to recognise your relationship.

Generally, in order to register a civil partnership, you can complete some forms at the registry of births, deaths and marriages. You can go through the registration process either with a declaration ceremony or by simply completing the forms without a ceremony.

You must be at least eighteen years or older and at least one of the parties to the relationship must live in the state where you are registering your relationship.

You may choose to register your relationship if you decide to continue in a de facto relationship but need some form of proof of your relationship. The registering of your relationship will make it easier for you to prove your relationship for things such as superannuation, tax and government payments. It will also be evidence, in the event that you separate later, that your de facto relationship existed.

When you apply to be married, you must give notice of your intention to marry thirty days prior to your marriage ceremony, and there is a similar requirement with a civil partnership. If you decide to have a civil partnership ceremony, the ceremony cannot take place until ten days after you have given notice of your intention to register your relationship. If you register your relationship without a ceremony, then the certificate will not issue for ten days after you lodge your application.

Marriage

Marriage is defined as **the union of two people to the exclusion of all others, voluntarily entered into for life**.

Aside from being a celebration of your relationship and let's face it, a good excuse to get friends and family together for a party, there are some essential elements to ensure that your marriage is valid.

Marriages must be solemnised by authorised celebrants. These are usually ministers of religion or a registered celebrant. The minister or celebrant must be duly authorised to carry out and register marriages.

Notice must be given, at least one month, but not more than eighteen months, prior to your wedding/marriage. This notice must be provided to your celebrant or minister so that they can prepare the required notice of intention and lodge that with the registry of births, deaths and marriages in your state or territory.

There must be two witnesses to the marriage who are over the age of eighteen years present at the time of the ceremony. This is usually an easy step in circumstances where a couple have a wedding party, traditionally including groomsmen and bridesmaids. In recent times we have seen the inclusion of extended friends and family in the witnessing requirements. The siblings who are not in the bridal party are sometimes called on to witness the paperwork.

The minister or celebrant will prepare the required marriage certificate and send the documents to the registry of births, deaths, and marriages for registration after the marriage.

Divorce and remarriage

One issue which comes up from time to time is re-marriage following the end of a relationship. It is important to know that **your divorce order must have been finalised prior to your marriage**. It is illegal to be married to more than one person at one time in Australia. Even though you have been separated for a long period of time, if you have not formally applied for a divorce, then your marriage to the first person has not formally ended. The end of a marriage is through an Application for Divorce. At the divorce hearing your divorce order is granted, however, it doesn't become final until one month and one day after the hearing. This is important to remember if you are planning your marriage date and have not yet formally divorced.

Case Study

Sarah had been married to Jasper for ten years. They separated three years ago and finalised their property settlement. Sarah thought this meant that she had also ended her marriage by divorce. She started to plan her new life including an upcoming marriage to Ben. Sarah contacted us for advice to make sure everything was finalised with her settlement so she could remarry. She explained that she had a financial agreement and that had concluded everything.

We explained to Sarah that her marriage and divorce were separate to her property settlement. Sarah asked us for assistance so that we could help finalise the divorce. Given the time that had passed we needed to locate Jasper and send him a copy of the divorce application. We finalised that process and waited for the court date. Sarah went about preparing for her upcoming wedding. We had explained to Sarah that her divorce would be finalised one month after her divorce hearing, however, in her excitement Sarah picked a wedding date inside the one month and one day timeframe. This would mean her marriage to Ben would be invalid.

We made a special application to the registrar on the day of the hearing to have the timeframe shortened to fourteen days. The registrar granted this request and Sarah was able to marry Ben on her chosen day.

This doesn't always happen, and the registrar has a discretion about whether to allow the time to be shortened.

Another occasion on which we have asked for a registrar to consider shortening the time was where our client was in a relationship with a terminally ill lady and they wanted to marry sooner rather than later. In that matter the time was shortened to seven days.

If you are remarrying, it is important to know that when you apply for a divorce having completed all of the necessary paperwork, on the day that your divorce order is heard by a registrar of the court, the divorce order will be granted but it will not become final until one month and one day following the divorce hearing. What this means is for example, that if your divorce hearing was on 12 September, then you are not free to marry another person until after 13 October in that year.

If you have been in a previous relationship and were married to that person and are now considering marrying another, then you need to make sure that you have this process sorted out so that there are no hiccups with your new marriage and your special day can go ahead without distress.

Changing your name

If you want to change your surname after you marry, **the process is relatively straight forward**. You need to obtain a certified extract of your marriage certificate from the registry of births, deaths and marriages – this is the formal extract from the registry and is different to ceremonial certificate that you receive on your wedding day.

You can find information about your local registry of births, deaths and marriages in the Resources section at the end of this book.

You will need to complete an application form and then go through a process to confirm your identify. Only certain people are allowed to apply for a copy of your marriage certificate.

There is a nominal fee to be paid to the registry.

Once you have that certified extract you can go to Queensland Transport, or the transport department in your state or territory and get a new driver's licence in your married name. Once you have changed your licence, you have changed your primary form of identification. You can then use your licence to change other things such as bank accounts, phone accounts and the like.

The process for updating your passport is a little more involved. The Australian Government will require the certified extract of your marriage certificate as they will need to formally track the change in name and assure themselves of the validity of the request. Here you are likely to need your birth certificate and your marriage certificate before applying for a new passport. If you have previously been married, you will also need your first marriage certificate and divorce order as well.

Traditionally, a wife changed her surname to her husband's, but nowadays there are more options.

- A husband may adopt his wife's surname
- A husband and wife may formally hyphenate both their names (not just the names of their children)
- Neither party may change their name and they may continue having different surnames.

The more complicated changes to names are lodged through the registry of births, deaths and marriages. In these circumstances you need to set out in the application form the reasons why you wish to change your name. Some examples which we have seen in recent times include the following:

- A de-facto wife decided to take her de-facto husband's surname in a long-term relationship. The parties in this matter ultimately married, though several years after the wife had already changed her name.
- A young man had three first names which were in a different order on various documents such as his licence, passport and bank accounts, with his third name being the name used in everyday life. An application was made to correct the order of his names to reflect how he was actually known.
- A young woman keen to forge her own path adopted her middle name as her surname.

It is certainly a case of 'each to their own' and whichever scenario applies to you, the process is straightforward.

What about the kids

The aim of this chapter is to provide practical advice and insights that will help you navigate the complexities of starting a new relationship where children from previous relationships are involved. It is not a chapter about whether you should have children in your new relationship, though if you do make that decision, the pages in this chapter are relevant to the dynamics in your household if one or both of you have children from prior relationships.

Going through a divorce or separation can be a challenging and emotional experience for everyone involved, especially children. As a lawyer who has worked with families going through this process, I understand the importance of putting the children's needs first and ensuring they have the support they need as they go through this difficult time.

But what happens when you decide to move on and start a new relationship? How do you navigate the complex dynamics of blending families to create a functional and loving environment for all involved?

This chapter will delve into the science and psychology behind what children go through when their parents separate. We'll explore general attachment theory and how it applies to children so you can better understand their needs and how to address them.

We'll discuss the importance of developing your new relationship around your children's needs and the dynamics that come into play when two sets of blended children come together.

Managing a household with children from different families can be challenging. That is why we'll provide tips for making it work. We'll also delve into the hush-hush topic of step-parent boundaries and behaviour, and how to navigate a smooth parenting relationship with the ex.

With this chapter, I want to empower you to create a happy and healthy family dynamic that prioritises the wellbeing of all family members. So, let's get right into it!

IMPACTS OF SEPARATION ON CHILDREN

When parents separate, it can be a traumatic experience for children, particularly if the process is not managed well by their parents or there are complex dynamics at play, including family violence. Children may experience various emotions, such as fear, anger, sadness and confusion. Throw in a new relationship, new house and new living arrangements and **it can be a stressful time for children** who will be worried about how all of these new things (including your relationship) will impact them or their other parent. It is a lot of change all at once. Acknowledging and validating what is going on for your child or children and supporting children as they navigate this difficult time is important.

In this section, we'll explore the emotional impact of separation on children, so that you can be on the look out for any concerns as you navigate your new relationship, and look into how to communicate effectively with children about the changes occurring.

The emotional impact of separation on children

The emotional impact of separation on children can be profound and long-lasting. They may feel abandoned or rejected by one or both parents and blame themselves for the separation. Children may also feel torn between their parents, which can cause significant stress and anxiety.

The child's age and developmental stage significantly affect how they process and respond to the separation. Younger children may struggle with understanding what is happening and may regress in their behaviour or development. Older children may understand the situation better but still struggle with feelings of loss and grief and the practical implications of the separation, such as changing schools or living arrangements.

The Australian Institute of Family Studies (AIFS) has undertaken significant research in how the family law system impacts children and young people. According to the AIFS, children of divorced parents are more likely to experience mental-health problems such as anxiety and depression than those of non-divorced parents. The primary cause of this is the family unit disruption and the emotional stress and uncertainty that comes with divorce. Children may also feel caught in their parents' conflicts, leading to guilt, confusion and anxiety.

The above findings correlate with another study published in the Journal of Child Psychology and Psychiatry. This study also suggests that children whose parents have divorced may experience various mental-health issues, such as depression and low self-esteem. These issues can significantly impact a child's overall wellbeing and have lasting effects into adulthood if not addressed.

As a child experiences different emotions during separation and divorce, parents need to acknowledge and validate these emotions, as this can help the children feel heard and supported.

Parents can do this by listening to their children, expressing empathy and understanding, and reassuring them of their unconditional love and that the separation is in no way their fault.

It's also important for parents to be consistent and reliable in their interactions with their children because this can help provide a sense of stability and security during a time of significant change.

Let us look at other common impacts of separation on children.

Poor academic performance
Divorce is difficult for all family members. Trying to understand the changing dynamics in the family can distract and confuse children. This disruption in their daily focus may result in poor academic performance. If children are worried about what is going on at home, they are

likely to be distracted at school. The more distracted children are, the less likely they are to concentrate on their schoolwork. Keeping a close eye on how your children are going at school may give you an early indication if they are not coping with the separation.

Anger/Irritability

In some cases, children who are overwhelmed and unsure of how to respond to the effects of divorce may become angry or irritable. They could direct their rage at a variety of perceived causes.

Children going through a divorce may become angry at their parents, themselves, their friends and others. This anger dissipates after a few weeks for many children; however, if it persists, it is important to be aware that the divorce may have a lingering effect and may lead to destructive behaviour.

Disinterest in social activities

According to research, divorce can negatively impact children socially. Children whose parents are divorcing may have a more difficult time relating to others and have less social contact. Children may feel insecure and wonder if they are the 'only one in the world' who is going through divorce.

In summary, **the emotional impact of separation on children can be significant**. For this reason, having an understanding of these dynamics when you introduce a new partner is vitally important. With support and understanding from parents and other caregivers, children can navigate this difficult time and come out stronger on the other side.

Now let's look at how to communicate effectively with children about the changes that are taking place.

HOW TO TALK TO KIDS ABOUT SEPARATION & DIVORCE

Regardless of whether you are starting a new relationship or it is still early days after your separation, effective communication with children about the changes occurring during separation or divorce is crucial to helping them understand and cope.

Here are some tips for communicating effectively.

Be honest

Children can sense when something is off; they also need time to understand what is happening to start processing their emotions. Be truthful and provide age-appropriate information.

Be clear

Use simple and clear language when discussing the changes taking place. Avoid using complex legal terms or information that is too difficult for children to understand.

Be respectful

Choose your words carefully, especially when you are talking about the other parent. Whilst not all family dynamics are the same, and in certain circumstances the separation will have come about due to family violence or other safety issues, the other parent is still the other parent and usually an important person for the child. **Be respectful of the other parent, regardless of the circumstances, and protect the children from any animosity you may be feeling.** Remember your children are already carrying their own response to the separation and do not need to be burdened by your response and feelings.

Be supportive

Reassure them of your unconditional love for them and ensure they know the separation is not their fault. Provide a safe and supportive environment where they can express their emotions without fear of judgement.

Listen actively

Encourage your children to express their feelings and listen to what they say. Acknowledge their emotions and validate their experiences.

Provide structure

Children thrive on routine and structure, especially during times of change. Try to maintain a sense of normalcy as much as possible and create a predictable schedule for children to follow. If you can continue your pre-separation routine for the children, they will more readily adjust to the changes that are unfolding.

By communicating effectively with children about the changes, parents can help alleviate some of the stress and confusion children may feel during separation.

GENERAL ATTACHMENT THEORY

Attachment theory is a psychological concept that explains the emotional bond or attachment between an infant and their primary caregiver. It was developed by John Bowlby, a British psychologist and ethologist.

According to the theory, infants are biologically programmed to seek proximity to their caregiver for safety and protection. The quality of the attachment between the infant and caregiver significantly impacts the child's emotional and social development.

Further studies show that the attachment bond between an infant and their caregiver forms through a series of interactions, such as feeding, comforting and playing.

At this point you may be wondering what this has to do with children, separation and new relationships. As parents it is important to understand what your children are going through as they transition between houses, meet new partners and cope generally with seeing their other parent less. **The younger your children are, the more time they will need to adjust.** Care needs to be taken with very young children not to rush or push for an arrangement which sees the children away from their primary parent for too long.

A child develops a secure attachment when their caregiver is consistently responsive and attuned to the infant's needs. In contrast, inconsistent or unresponsive caregiving can lead to insecure attachment, negatively affecting the child's emotional and social development. This negative impact on a child's development can have long lasting effects.

Attachment theory revolves around the idea that children need to feel safe and secure to develop and thrive. It suggests that children with a strong emotional bond with a caregiver are more likely to feel secure, confident and able to explore the world around them.

With this in mind, when you start a new relationship with children involved (whether they are your children or your partner's children), you can see why it's important to understand the role of attachment theory and how it can impact a child's emotional wellbeing. There is a lot of change happening all at once. A child may feel anxious or fearful about the new person in their parent's life, as this person may look like a threat to their secure attachment with the primary parent or caregiver.

As a parent, taking things slowly and building trust and rapport gradually between your children and any new partner is essential. Spend time with your children, gradually include your new partner, do things that interest your children and provide emotional support. Doing this can involve engaging in activities the child enjoys, such as playing games or reading books and listening to their concerns or questions about changes in their life.

It's also important to respect your children's boundaries and allow them to set the pace of the new relationship. Pushing too hard or trying to force a connection before they are ready can be counterproductive and damaging to the relationship over time.

By understanding these principles and taking a patient, compassionate approach to building a relationship between your children and your new partner, you can create a secure foundation for a healthy and fulfilling family dynamic.

Having understood the attachment theory and its impact, let us now see how you can navigate a new relationship when you have kids.

DEVELOPING YOUR NEW RELATIONSHIP

Whether you are the parent with children, or your new partner has children, or both, working out how children will meet a new partner is key in setting up a positive family dynamic from the outset. **Think about the timing**, have good open conversations with each other about what the introduction might look like, but don't put yourself under too much pressure so that the interaction feels staged! Make sure you are both on the same page and understand how the meeting will go to ensure smooth sailing for everyone.

It is also important to consider the other parent – that is, your child's other biological parent, particularly if they spend regular time with your child. Keep in mind that your children are likely to report back to the other parent anything new that is happening for them. If the co-parenting relationship with your ex allows, you should be in touch with them to give them a heads up. Whilst you might take the view that your new relationship is your business, an ex who is not caught by surprise is going to be far easier to deal with on a day to day basis.

Remember that bonds between children and new partners won't form immediately, be patient. Remember, only introduce a new partner to your children if it's serious; if it is, it'll be worth waiting for your child to come around on their own.

When starting a new relationship with children in the mix, it's important to **prioritise the kids' needs and create a family dynamic that works for everyone**. Doing this may involve adjusting your routines and schedules, communicating effectively with your partner and children, and building positive relationships between all family members.

This section will explore strategies for developing your new relationship around your children's needs and guide how to navigate potential challenges.

First, it is important to **ensure minimal or zero disruption in your children's daily routines**, such as school, extracurricular activities and time with friends.

One way to do this is by adjusting your routines and schedules to accommodate the needs of all family members. In practical, everyday life, this may involve coordinating with your partner and their children's other parent to create a schedule that works for everyone.

Another crucial aspect of developing your new relationship is communication. **Communicating effectively with your partner, your children and your ex** about the changes taking place and how you plan to navigate them as a family is vital. This may involve having open and honest conversations about everyone's feelings, concerns and needs.

Building positive relationships between all family members is also critical. This may involve finding activities everyone enjoys, such as playing board games, going out or cooking meals together. It's essential to create a sense of belonging and unity among all family members, including step-parents and stepchildren.

Navigating potential challenges is another aspect of developing your new relationship. This may involve dealing with conflict, managing jealousy or resentment and setting clear boundaries. It's important to **address any issues as they arise and seek outside support if necessary**, such as family counselling or therapy.

It may sound as though the children are the only priority, however in reality, they are not the only priority. Further, while it's important to listen to children and validate how they are feeling in this time of significant change, it is also important to remember that you are the parent and the adult – children still take direction from their parents and you shouldn't find yourself in a position where it feels like your children are in charge. It is a fine balance. When you are conscious of the dynamics at play you will be more readily able to deal with children who are pushing those boundaries.

In summary, developing your new relationship around your children's needs requires careful consideration, communication and a willingness to make adjustments as necessary.

By prioritising the wellbeing of all family members, you can create a stable and supportive environment that fosters positive relationships and healthy emotional development for everyone involved.

Some challenges may arise when developing a new relationship around your children's needs.

Here are some tips for navigating them.

Take things slow

Giving your children time to adjust to the new situation is important. Rushing into things can cause anxiety and stress for them. Take it one step at a time and gradually integrate your new partner into your family routine.

Communicate openly and honestly

Communicating with your partner and children about their feelings and concerns is crucial. Encourage open and honest communication to build trust and understanding.

Respect your children's feelings

Your children may have mixed emotions about the new relationship. Respect and try to understand their feelings and perspective. Don't force them to accept your partner or rush them into developing a relationship. Give them time and space to process their emotions.

Involve your children in the new relationship

Find ways to spend time with your children in your new relationship. This could be as simple as having family movie nights or going out together. It will help your children feel included and valued in the new family dynamic.

Be patient and flexible

Building a new family dynamic takes time, patience and flexibility. Be prepared to adjust your routines and schedules to accommodate everyone's needs.

Seek professional help if necessary

If you or your children struggle to adjust to the new situation, don't hesitate to seek professional help. A therapist or counsellor can provide guidance and support as you navigate this challenging time.

THE DYNAMICS OF BLENDED FAMILIES

So your relationship has developed, and now you feel it is time to include the kids in a more integrated way. How, then, do you go about it?

If you and your new partner both have children, it is important to consider the dynamics that will arise when the two families come together. An added factor to consider will be whether you and your new partner have children together.

Blended families can be complex and require careful management to ensure everyone feels included and valued. It's important to approach this process with patience and understanding and seek to create a family dynamic that allows everyone to feel heard and valued.

This section will cover the dynamics that may arise when two lots of children come together and provide guidance on navigating these challenges to promote positive relationships and a sense of belonging for all family members.

Before we look at the issues that may arise when two lots of children come together, let us get to know what a blended family is.

So, what is a blended family?

When you and your partner live with the children from one or both of your previous relationships, you form a blended or stepfamily family unit. If you decide to have children together, a further addition to the family unit occurs.

Now let us look at the issues that may arise when children from different family groups come together.

One common issue is **integrating the two families**. This can be a complicated process, especially when the children involved may have different backgrounds and lifestyles. Each member of the new family unit may have personal traditions, routines and expectations that can lead to conflicts and disagreements. It takes time and effort to integrate different family systems, and there may be resistance from some family members.

The **different types of parenting arrangement** for each family will also play a part in how the children cope with the new circumstances. Some parents are lucky enough to align their parenting arrangements so that these align for all children. Others are unable to do that, so some children are in the household when others are not. An added dynamic occurs when some children live permanently at one home and the other children may feel like they are just visiting that home.

Children may also feel torn between loyalty to their biological parent and their new step-parent. Acknowledging these feelings and creating a safe space for children to express their emotions is important. Encourage open communication between all family members and reassure children that loving and respecting both biological and step-parents is possible.

Communication can also be a major challenge in blended families, especially with different communication styles or language barriers. Family members must work on their communication skills and be open and honest about their thoughts, feelings and needs.

Role ambiguity can cause confusion and frustration, too, as the roles of each family member may be unclear or overlapping. For example, step-parents may struggle to balance being supportive and involved in their stepchildren's lives without overstepping boundaries or trying to replace the biological parent.

Blended families may also face **financial challenges**, such as child-support payments, shared expenses and the financial needs of multiple households. Families need to be transparent about their financial situation and work together to find solutions that work for everyone.

With two different families coming together, there may be **differences in household rules and expectations**. It's important to communicate openly with all family members about these differences and work together to create rules and expectations that everyone can agree on. It's also important to consistently enforce these rules and have consequences when individual family members fail to follow them.

Sometimes, children may resent their new step-siblings or struggle to adjust to the new family dynamic. **Be patient and understanding** and create opportunities for family members to spend quality time together. Encourage open communication and provide emotional support for children who may be struggling with the adjustment.

Another challenge may be managing the two families' parenting styles or disciplinary methods. It's important to communicate openly and honestly with your partner about these differences and work together to establish a consistent approach that works for everyone. Consider any agreements which were in place with your ex and ensure those same rules are applied.

Blending two families requires patience, understanding and a willingness to adapt to new circumstances. By prioritising communication, empathy and respect for each other's differences, it is possible to create a positive and fulfilling family dynamic that brings everyone closer together.

HOW TO BUILD HEALTHY BLENDED FAMILY RELATIONSHIPS

Building positive relationships between all family members in a blended family can take time and effort, but it's worth it for the wellbeing of everyone involved.

Here are some ways to foster positive relationships.

Set rules and expectations about how to treat each other

Establish clear expectations and rules about respecting each other's boundaries and personal space. This can include using polite language, being respectful during conversations and not interrupting each other.

Setting up these expectations and rules can create a positive and respectful environment for everyone in the family.

Provide each child with their own sanctuary

When blending families, ensuring each child has their own space and belongings can make a world of difference because it can help children feel more secure and less threatened by the new family dynamic. Encourage children to decorate and personalise their spaces to make them feel at home in their own space. This is especially important so that children who are in your household less regularly don't feel like they are simply visiting. You want for them to feel at home

Display photos of all children throughout the house

Photos of all children around the house can help create a sense of unity and inclusiveness. It can also show each child they are valued and important in the family. If it is appropriate and safe to do so, you should also display photos of you ex. This may be difficult, depending on the circumstances of your separation, however, remember that your ex is the other parent of your child and they are an important person for your child.

Find ways for children to have fun together

Blending families can be challenging, but encouraging children to have fun together can help build positive relationships. Plan family activities and outings that everyone can participate in and encourage children to get to know each other and bond over shared experiences.

Building positive relationships between all family members in a blended family takes time and effort. By establishing clear expectations, providing personal space, showing inclusiveness and encouraging fun and bonding, you can create a happy and harmonious family dynamic.

Tackling chores as a blended family

Two of the major challenges of blending members of different households are chores and expectations of what everyone should do.

No one wants to become the stereotypical evil stepmother from the fairy tales who makes her stepchildren wear rags and clean the floors while her real children party and eat candy. This long-standing generalisation may contribute to the sensitivity around household chores in blended families.

In reality, chores can be a helpful tool for parents. In addition to instilling a sense of responsibility and the ability to contribute to the home's upkeep, chores are a tangible reminder that every one of you is an integral part of the larger family unit.

Here are some tips to help navigate this challenge.

Talk to your partner first

Being a step-parent means joining a family that began with a completely different parenting arrangement. As a result, your stepchildren may have grown up in a household with different expectations from yours. Before allocating duties, talk with your partner and ensure you are on the same page.

In a best-case scenario, you will be able to consult with the other parent and devise a chore plan that works for both houses. This keeps things consistent for the youngsters all around. If that's not an option, strive for consistency in your home.

Establish clear expectations

Establish clear expectations and rules around household chores, routines and responsibilities because it can help avoid confusion and conflict later. For example, who is responsible for cooking dinner? Who will do the laundry? Clear expectations can help everyone feel supported and contribute to a positive family dynamic.

Assign chores based on time in the house

While expectations should be the same for all children, the number of times a duty is completed may vary. For example, if one of the chores on the list is to make the bed every day, the kids should do so every day in the house, even if that means making their bed more than the other kids.

If the duty is to do the dishes once or twice a week, don't make the kids who are only present on weekends do them every weekend; instead, create a rotation that feels equitable for everyone. Everything should start flowing more smoothly around the house once everyone starts pitching in.

Encourage open communication

Communication is key in any family, but it's especially important in blended families where there may be more individuals and relationships to manage.

Encourage open communication between all family members and create a safe and supportive environment where everyone feels comfortable sharing their thoughts and feelings.

Consider the needs of all family members

Blended families often involve children of different ages and backgrounds. It's important to consider the needs of all family members when managing the household.

For example, younger children may need more support with homework and bedtime routines, while teenagers may need more independence and privacy.

Be flexible

Blended families can be dynamic and ever-changing. Being flexible and adaptable can help to navigate the challenges that arise. For example, if one family member needs to change their schedule or routine, be open to finding a solution that works for everyone.

Managing a blended family household can be challenging, but creating a positive and supportive family dynamic is possible with patience, open communication and flexibility.

STEP-PARENT BOUNDARIES AND CO-PARENTING

Blended families can be fantastic for children, with some step-parents becoming as important as biological parents. However, this does not imply it will be easy for you, your new partner, or your children.

Co-parenting with a new partner is one of the challenges many divorced or single parents encounter when raising their children. Giving someone who is not their biological parent some responsibility for your children's wellbeing can be difficult, and young children may struggle to respect their authority.

That is why you must establish limits and guarantee everyone involved feels content with the new co-parenting arrangement.

When you find a new partner as a divorced parent, you need to take care of three relationships.

The first relationship is with **the other biological parent**. Even though they might not be your spouse, you still have a relationship with them and must consider their opinions when making parenting decisions. A successful transition into co-parenting in new relationships depends on establishing goodwill from the outset and maintaining that.

Your new partner is the second relationship in your life. They could be struggling with adding a child to their family, so you need to keep them content with the new dynamic.

Your bond with **your child** is the most crucial and lasting one. The dynamic ensures that you, your ex and your new partner contribute to your child's happiness. We'll talk more about how to navigate co-parenting later, but it's vital to always to remember your child.

Of course, **you must also maintain your happiness** in addition to the happiness of these three people. You must ensure your priorities include you because you are equally essential. While co-parenting, each connection must be strong and inclusive of all parties, consider each person and their behavioural impact while establishing limits.

Let's discuss how you can establish good boundaries with your new spouse.

Consult with your ex-partner

When bringing a new partner into the parenting dynamic, it is important to keep your ex informed about that. The extent of that consulting will depend on the type of parenting relationship you have and how involved that parent is with the children. Mostly, unless there are serious parenting capacity issues or family violence, both parents generally need to make joint decisions about the arrangements for your children. For that reason it is important that you talk to your ex before you introduce your new partner to give them a heads up. As I've said earlier, it's much easier to get along with a parent who isn't taken by surprise.

It's important to discuss with your ex-partner how they plan to handle time with the children and how any new spouse will be involved in their routines. This discussion will help ensure there are no misunderstandings or conflicts and that everyone is on the same page.

You can start by asking your ex about their plans for parenting time with the children and how they see their new spouse fitting into that time. Respecting your ex's wishes and preferences while ensuring your child's needs and feelings are a key consideration is important.

You can also discuss how the children will interact with your ex's new spouse during their time together. This can include setting boundaries around discipline, routines and expectations.

For example, if a new partner is not comfortable disciplining the children, it may be helpful to establish clear rules and consequences everyone can follow.

It's also important to keep communication open with your ex about any issues or concerns that may arise during their parenting time. This can help ensure that any issues receive prompt and effective solutions and that everyone works together to provide the best possible environment for the children.

Remember, co-parenting can be challenging, especially when new partners are involved. However, staying open and communicative with your ex-partner and their new spouse can help build a positive and supportive environment for everyone involved.

Talk to your child

Your child should be the primary focus of your attention. Never try to impose a romantic relationship on your children; instead, have a conversation with them before bringing a new partner into their lives.

It's not that you shouldn't date if your child isn't thrilled about it; you just shouldn't try to force them into liking the new person or spending time with them before they are ready. Do things carefully and include the children as much as possible when they're ready and agreeable.

Begin with a simple get-together with your child at a park or another familiar setting. Make sure they know they are still your top priority and give them time to adjust to your new partner before letting them into your house.

Consider how your child is feeling and communicate with your partner about your child's emotions. If your child is old enough you might talk to them about the situation, see how they are feeling, what they are thinking about your new relationship. Ultimately you are the adult and you will need to make a decision that is best for you and your family.

Get their thoughts on the future of their relationship with your new significant other and what things your new partner could do that would be too much for your child.

Know your boundaries

While co-parenting, it's natural to consider the other parent's needs. But remember that your preferences matter, too. Consider the role your new spouse would like to play as a parent and how involved you'd like them to be with your kids.

Here are some questions to ask to establish personal limits:

- Would you be comfortable leaving your children with your new partner?
- Would you mind if your partner disciplined your children?
- Do you want your new partner to attend school meetings about your children?
- Do you plan to listen to your new partner's advice on parenting?

It's important to consider the role you hope your new companion will play in your life. Is it fair to let them live with you and your child if you aren't satisfied with the strong parental role they are taking?

Be transparent with your new partner

It's important to be open and honest with your partner about the role your children have in your life. Ensure they understand your child's significance and that they take precedence. If they cannot understand this perspective, it might be time to reconsider the viability of the relationship. However, it's also vital to reassure them that their presence is valued and wanted, and dedicated effort will be made to nurture your relationship.

Consider your new partner's wishes

Remember that not every partner will want to engage with your child. Some may be thrilled at the prospect of embracing a new family and becoming a terrific step-parent, while others may be frightened or unprepared. Before you proceed, discuss how your partner feels and tell them what you expect.

This is the time to synchronise your thoughts so you're all on the same page. If your partner is willing to become a co-parent and participate, you can move on to creating boundaries. If they aren't, consider devising a solution, including living apart until your partner is ready to play a more involved role.

Establish boundaries with discipline

One of the most difficult limits to manage is discipline. Every parent has their unique method of disciplining their child, and you must ensure your partner knows your regulations. Otherwise, chaos is unavoidable!

Explain the negative behaviour you are looking to address in your child. For example, where applicable you may limit the child's TV time and have a system to reprimand them if they have tantrums over wanting to watch more. The important message here is to understand that that your new spouse will not know how to treat your child in these situations, and you will have to teach them your approach.

You should also learn about your partner's disciplining methods if your partner has children.

If you're living together, you must agree on what behaviour is and isn't actionable and the consequences for specific behaviours. This is essential to provide a fair atmosphere for your children.

If your partner does not have children, talk about how involved your new partner will be in disciplining your child. Ensure your partner is well prepared to enact your discipline plan for the kids when you are not around but initially restrict your partner's input until things have settled into a routine. A strict partner forcing new restrictions on your child will likely lead to conflict, so avoid this if you are uncomfortable.

What information to share about your child

Co-parents frequently need to disclose much information about their child, so ensure you're okay with this. If your new partner is involved in your child's life, you must keep them updated. If you're concerned about forgetting, use a calendar to keep them informed and feel included.

Should your new partner be included if you already use co-parenting tools with your ex? To avoid arguments, talk to your ex before permitting your new partner to use the tools. You can find a list of commonly used parenting communication applications in the resources section at the end of the book.

Communication

When learning how to co-parent, communication is very important. As you go on this adventure together, check in with each other regularly to assess what's working and what isn't. You should also maintain regular conversations with your child to ensure they are comfortable with the new dynamic and do not wish to make any changes.

TIPS FOR A HAPPY BLENDED FAMILY

Now that the boundaries are in place, let's discuss the tips for creating a happy blended family.

Creating a happy blended family can be challenging, but it's possible with effort and commitment.

Here are some tips to help:

Communication is key: Open and honest communication is vital in any relationship, especially in a blended family. Encourage everyone to share their feelings and concerns and work together to find solutions that work for everyone.

Respect each other's boundaries: Each person in the family has unique needs and boundaries. Respecting these boundaries and working together to find a compromise that works for everyone is important.

Set realistic expectations: Blending families takes time, and it's important to set realistic expectations for how quickly things will progress. Be patient and understanding, and celebrate small victories along the way.

Spend quality time together: Making time for family activities and bonding can help to strengthen the family bond. Plan activities everyone can enjoy, such as game nights, movie nights, or outdoor adventures.

Seek support when needed: Blended families can be challenging, and it's important to seek support when needed. Consider joining a support group or seeking the help of a family therapist.

By following these tips and being committed to creating a happy blended family, building a strong and loving family unit that can weather any challenge is possible.

In conclusion, navigating co-parenting and step-parenting can be a challenging and complex experience. It requires a willingness to communicate openly, establish boundaries and build positive relationships with all family members involved. Understanding attachment theory and the emotional needs of children can provide a helpful framework for creating a healthy and supportive family environment.

It's important to prioritise the wellbeing of the children and ensure their needs come first. This includes involving the other biological parent in discussing introducing a new partner and respecting their boundaries and opinions. It's also important to establish clear expectations and rules for all family members to create a sense of stability and security.

Creating a happy blended family takes time and effort, but it's possible with patience, communication and a willingness to work together. Families can thrive in their new dynamics by setting boundaries, encouraging positive interactions between children and building a foundation of mutual respect and understanding.

Apples and Oranges

In this section we will cover the assets – your property, debts, super-annuation and other assets – which you will acquire during or bring into your relationship.

People start relationships from varying stages of life.

You may be in the **everything is new phase**. If you are younger, you may be focused on exploring new experiences and figuring out who you are, which can affect what you're looking for in a relationship. You may have limited assets or what might feel like just debt.

You may have been focused on your career for several years and now ready to find love in the **I've worked hard now it's time for love phase**. You will be keen to ensure that any wealth you have grown is protected and that your relationship is based on foundations of similar goals.

You may be recently or not so recently separated or divorced and cautious about any new adventure with love in the **I've been through this before phase**. You are likely to be keen to protect yourself from the separation or divorce process and make strategic decisions about how you go into any new relationship.

Wherever you find yourself in your relationship journey, there are important conversations to be had and legal considerations to be aware of.

WHEN 'ME' BECOMES 'WE'

When you commence a new relationship, regardless of where you are in life, financial matters can become a source of stress and conflict if not addressed proactively. It is important to consider the following questions about arrangements:

- Will you have a joint account, sole accounts or a combination? Deciding whether to have joint accounts or keep finances separate is a personal decision that should be made based on individual circumstances and preferences. It's important to have a clear understanding of each partner's financial responsibilities and to establish a system for managing joint finances.

- How will your incomes be used? Who will pay for what?
- Does one partner earn more income than the other? Be realistic about income.
- What's your approach to money? Be on the same page about spending and saving.
- How will debts be managed? Do one or both partners have credit card debts, student loans or car loans?
- Where will you live? Are you moving into a new property together or a property already owned or rented by one party. Are you living together rent free or at a reduced rent with parents?

When in a committed relationship, it's important to **consider future financial goals and planning** to ensure that both partners are on the same page regarding finances. Here you could be thinking about the following:

- Acquiring property together – how you might do that, what each of you will contribute financially, whether you will own property as joint tenants or have different shares depending on the contributions you each make.
- If one party owns property, determine how or if the other party contributes to the on-going costs of running and maintaining the property.
- Setting some savings goals for big-ticket items, such as a home, a car or a wedding, can help ensure that both partners are working together towards a shared goal.

- Think about future investments – investing in stocks, bonds or real estate can help grow wealth over time, but it's important to have a clear understanding of each others risk tolerance and investment goals.

MUM AND DAD WILL PAY FOR THE WEDDING AND OTHER GIFT STORIES

It is not uncommon for parents to make substantial gifts of housing deposits to one or both parties in a relationship. Parents also make financial contributions to weddings and other celebrations. This **assistance by parents is becoming more common** in recent years with the impact of the affordability of the property market.

There are relevant legal principles to understand when considering how a significant financial contribution from a parent will be considered. Generally, a gift from a parent is deemed to be a contribution for the benefit of that parent's child unless there is evidence which shows the intention was to benefit both parties to the relationship.

Case Study

Sarah and Rachel were high-school sweethearts. Their relationship continued and after five years Sarah and Rachel married. As their relationship progressed, they were keen to purchase a property together in their local community. Rachel's parents had been wanting to subdivide their property for some time, as the size of that property was becoming too much for them to manage. In recognition of their marriage, Rachel's parents gifted a parcel of land to Sarah and Rachel. Both Sarah and Rachel's names appeared on the title registered for the property.

Unfortunately things don't work out for Sarah and Rachel and after 10 years together they separated. If Rachel's parents had transferred the property to Rachel only, the argument would be that the gift was for Rachel's benefit and a contribution on Rachel's behalf.

Here, where the gifted property is in both names, there is an argument available that the intention of the gift was to benefit both Sarah and Rachel. It is important to note, however, that courts have held that a gift of property which is registered in the parties' joint names has been held to only benefit the daughter of the parent where the court, considered that the gift was made only because the relationship existed and, in reality, it was a means of benefiting their daughter.

How contributions to the property are made after the gift will still be relevant. If the other party makes financial or physical contributions to that property during the relationship, that will ultimately impact any future property division.

Another relevant factor in relationships is whether money provided by parents or third parties is a **gift or a loan**. Oftentimes in a divorce, there can be a change in the characterisation of a gift to a loan which the party whose parent provided the funds now insists is a loan that both parties must repay. There is a need for caution here. If the monies are, in fact, a loan, make sure there is a loan agreement in place, that the funds given are intended to be repaid, and that repayments are made.

As will be seen in the next section, these are the types of significant money events where retaining documents relevant to the transaction will be essential.

WHY DOCUMENTS ARE IMPORTANT

It is essential to retain important documents in relationships. Aside from assisting in building trust, they can also protect both partners' legal and financial interests in the future.

Retaining documents can **promote transparency and open communication** in a new relationship. By sharing important documents, partners can establish trust and build a strong foundation for a healthy and fulfilling relationship.

Important financial documents such as bank statements, tax returns and insurance policies can help partners manage their finances effectively. By retaining these documents, both partners can keep track of their financial obligations and work together to manage their finances effectively.

Retaining essential documents can also help with future planning, such as retirement or estate planning. By having access to these documents, both partners can work together to plan for the future and ensure their financial needs and goals are met.

From a legal perspective, there are several reasons why you should keep relevant documents in a safe space. Important documents such as prenuptial agreements, wills and trusts are legal documents that provide legal protection for both partners. By retaining these documents, both partners can ensure that their wishes are carried out and that their assets are protected in the event of divorce or death.

Considering your relationship from a family law perspective, **documents are crucial to providing evidence about the financial status of your relationship** in the event of separation or divorce. While by no means should you embark on your relationship thinking it will all end someday and that you better keep all of your documents in order, making a plan for documents and keeping relevant documents stored in a safe place will mean that if that time comes, you will have all the information you need.

What are relevant documents? The Family Law Act requires that parties disclose documents relevant to a fact in issue. That means that if you received an inheritance of $80,000 in the third year of your ten-year de facto relationship, that might be a fact that needs proving. A copy of the will, the letter from the solicitor and a bank statement showing receipt of those funds into your account will be relevant documents. How you spent the money will also be relevant.

Another example may be the purchase of your first home together. If one party uses their savings for the deposit, bank statements, money transfers to the solicitor's trust account, the contract and settlement statement may be relevant documents.

If you aren't sure about whether a document is necessary or may become significant, it is best to be cautious and file a copy away. Ask yourself – is this an important financial event in our relationship? If the answer is yes, keep the documents.

PROTECTING WHAT YOU HAVE

Entering into a financial agreement either before or during your marriage or de facto relationship allows you to formalise the arrangements which would be put into place in the event of a subsequent separation.

You may commonly know these types of agreements to be prenuptial agreements or a 'prenup', though the Family Law Act formally calls these documents **financial agreements**.

A financial agreement before or during your relationship, when properly prepared, has the effect of contracting out of your right to later bring an application for property settlement under the Family Law Act. As a private agreement, a financial agreement does not require registration or approval of the court.

'Contract out of your right' means that you are setting out in your financial agreement what you say happens if you separate, regardless of what the law says you might be entitled to. When you come to the end of your relationship, if the agreement is valid, you have no right to bring a claim under the Family Law Act to seek a different outcome.

Why would you need a financial agreement?

There are a range of circumstances which might lead you to consider entering into a financial agreement with your spouse. They can be particularly useful under the following circumstances:

- you and your partner are in significantly unequal financial positions at the beginning of your relationship
- you want clarity or peace of mind about how your property would be divided if your relationship ends
- you may wish to protect specific property from any future property division, whether a business interest, inheritance or trust
- you may have children from a prior relationship whom you wish to provide for.

Why do financial agreements seem so expensive to prepare?

As mentioned earlier, a financial agreement provides you with the opportunity to 'contract out of your right' to have the family law courts later determine any property settlement. It is for that reason that the Family Law Act places **strict requirements on how the agreement must be prepared**, strict obligations on parties to provide accurate information and provide full disclosure of their affairs, and strict obligations on legal advisors to provide appropriate advice regarding the advantages and disadvantages of entering into the agreement and the effect of the agreement on your rights.

For a financial agreement to be binding, it must fulfil the following criteria:

- it must be in writing
- it must be signed by all parties
- before signing the agreement, each party must receive advice from a legal practitioner about the effects of the agreement on the rights of the party and the advantages and disadvantages of entering into the agreement at the time the advice is required
- before or after signing the agreement, each party must receive a signed statement by the legal practitioner confirming that the above advice was provided with a copy of the statement provided to the other party or their lawyer
- the agreement has not been terminated by further agreement or set aside by the court.

Due to the nature of a financial agreement, there is a **significant amount of work that goes into the preparation** to make sure that these strict requirements and obligations are complied with and to ensure that the financial agreement is binding and protects your interests.

What's the point? Can't a financial agreement just be set aside anyway?

A well-prepared financial agreement should stand up to any challenge down the track. This is why so much care is taken in getting the agreement prepared correctly in the first place. **Some things that can go wrong** are as follows:

- **The agreement is rushed** and prepared as parties are 'walking down the aisle'. This type of agreement causes a number of concerns. The biggest is that of duress. Many of the cases which have overturned a financial agreement arose when one party was under significant pressure to sign the agreement. That party feels like they have no option but to sign the agreement, otherwise the relationship is over. If there is a significant level of distress and duress, then a financial agreement can be set aside.

- **Not all of the financial assets have been disclosed.** A financial agreement can be set aside if it comes out later that there were significant assets not disclosed by one party. Each party to the agreement is entitled to know the complete financial position of the other before finalising the agreement. Disclosure of all assets is a significant part of the financial agreement process. If all of the details are not known or it turns out later that there were significant assets that one party didn't know about, then the agreement can be set aside.

- **The legal advice received is inadequate.** As lawyers, we have an obligation to provide parties to the agreement with legal advice. This is a legal obligation. It means as lawyers we must do it, and there is no getting around that process. Lawyers must give you advice about the advantages and disadvantages of entering into the agreement and the effect of the agreement on a party's rights. This means that the lawyer must give you advice about your expected entitlement and what would the likely outcome be if you had been in the relationship for a period of time, separate and have no agreement; or what happens if you have children in the future. If one party does not receive adequate legal advice, the agreement can be set aside.

Other reasons where a financial agreement can be set aside are the following:

- where the agreement was obtained by fraud (including non-disclosure of a material matter)
- where the agreement was entered into for the purposes of defeating or defrauding a creditor
- where the agreement was entered into for the purposes of defeating or defrauding a spouse
- where the agreement is void, voidable or unenforceable
- where the agreement or part of the agreement is now impractical to be carried out
- where since making the agreement, there has been a material change in circumstances (relating to the care of a child of the relationship) which would cause the applicant to suffer hardship if the agreement is not set aside
- where a party has engaged in unconscionable conduct
- where there are affected superannuation interests.

The test for duress is a high threshold to meet. It is not sufficient for one party to feel that the only option was to sign financial agreement or there would not be a wedding. See the following case study to understand how a court might consider the argument of duress.

Case Study

When she met Harry, Isobel was thirty-six years old, had no children and no assets of substance. Harry was sixty-seven. He had significant assets of at least $18 million, and three adult children from an earlier marriage.

Isobel and Harry met on a dating site. They fell in love. They travelled together and decided to marry. After returning to Australia, Harry attended his lawyer and arranged for a financial agreement. The lawyer later gave evidence that Harry's view was that the marriage would only go ahead if Isobel signed a financial agreement. Over the following weeks, the financial agreement was prepared. Isobel met with a lawyer for advice regarding the agreement, and the lawyer advised Isobel not to go through with the agreement. Isobel signed it anyway and the parties then married.

After around five years together, Harry and Isobel decided to separate. Isobel filed an application seeking property settlement. She said she had no option but to sign the financial agreement, that she was under duress and that was why she went ahead with it.

Isobel argued that she knew there would be no wedding if she didn't sign the agreement. She loved Harry. She wanted a wedding. She wanted a child with Harry. She changed her whole life and moved to Australia to be with Harry. Harry's position was plain. The terms were clear. There was no negotiation. Harry's view was no agreement, no wedding and no relationship. Isobel knew this.

Isobel felt powerless in these negotiations. She had no financial assistance, she was in Australia, away from her home, and she relied on Harry for all things. She argued that the agreement was signed under duress.

The test for duress is whether there is 'threatened or actual unlawful conduct'. There needs to be a finding by the court that there was pressure which was illegitimate or unlawful. It is not sufficient for pressure to simply be overwhelming. There must be more than an absence of choice.

Here, there is no doubt that Isobel was reliant on Harry both financially and emotionally. Isobel looked to Harry to look after her and he did. It is difficult to say that there was illegitimate or unlawful pressure by Harry. Ultimately the main difficulty for Isobel in establishing duress was that she took advice from her lawyer and her lawyer advised her not to sign the document. Regardless of that advice, she went ahead and signed the financial agreement.

While there are ways that a financial agreement can be set aside, it is not a simple process. A party needs to prove that one of the above things has happened. If there is no agreement, then an application to court is required. If a party is not successful, there are cost consequences that flow.

FINANCIAL AGREEMENTS – WHAT IS THE PROCESS?

While the process will be tailored to each individual client, there are generally standard steps which must be taken to ensure that the agreement prepared is binding and protects both parties in the future. Read on to learn more about what the process involves.

Initial appointment

It is important that you meet with your lawyer before going ahead with a financial agreement. Your lawyer needs to understand the circumstances of how you come to be looking at an agreement, the circumstances of your relationship and what you understand about how the agreement works. Your lawyer will also be able to tell you whether it is a good step for you to take and some of the reasons why it may or may not be in your interests to go ahead with the agreement.

Detailed cost assessment with client agreement

After you have met with your lawyer, they are in a position to give you a detailed costs assessment. Each financial agreement is tailored to your particular circumstances, so it is not possible to simply give an 'on the spot' quote for the work to be done without knowing you and what you are trying to achieve. Your matter might be far more complicated or even far less complicated than you first imagined.

Your lawyer must send you detailed costs assessment with their client agreement. These documents will set out the work that is necessary to assist you in your matter. Upon your acceptance of the client agreement, your lawyer will be able to proceed with assisting you with your agreement.

Detailed instructions and disclosure

This is a key part of the process. It takes time. Ensuring that your lawyer has your instructions recorded properly and all relevant disclosure has been reviewed and exchanged is vital to ensuring that your agreement is binding. There are certain circumstances which can later lead a court to set aside the agreement.

Disclosure

A court can set aside a financial agreement where there has been non-disclosure of a material matter – that is, if interests in property, whether assets, liabilities, superannuation, income or other financial resources were not properly disclosed during the preparation of the agreement, a court may set the agreement aside.

The details of all interests in property, assets, liabilities, superannuation and the like are all recorded in detail in the financial agreement. By signing the agreement, you each declare that those are the interests in property held by you at that point in time.

It is for these reasons that it is imperative that all relevant documents be disclosed and exchanged with each other. If there are properties or share portfolios and investments, they should be valued. Bank statements showing current balances should be exchanged. It is risky to enter into a financial agreement simply on the basis that you both have a 'pretty good idea' of the financial details for each other.

Voluntary agreement

The agreement must be entered into voluntarily, free from duress. There are many reported cases about 'prenups' being signed on the way to the altar with the distressed party often successful in arguing that they were under duress to sign the agreement.

If you are considering entering into a financial agreement, you should allow plenty of time for discussions, disclosure, advice and signing. Rushing only increases the risk of one party feeling that they are signing under pressure and therefore the risk of having the agreement set aside.

Drafting the agreement

A properly drafted financial agreement should, as far as possible, consider all foreseeable scenarios having regard to your current financial circumstances and present future intentions. It is for this reason it takes time, both for your lawyer to draft the agreement and for both parties to review and consider the agreement.

A financial agreement is not a document that can be whipped up with any haste. Clauses are included within the agreement to protect you from, for example, matters such as disclosure or the timing of the agreement which could cause the agreement to be set aside. The agreement which you reach with your partner about how your property is to be divided on separation is set out in detail including who is to take what step, when and how.

Advising about the agreement

Once the financial agreement has been finalised and both parties agree to the terms then your lawyer should provide you with a detailed letter of advice to meet strict obligations as legal advisors. In particular, the Family Law Act says for an agreement to be binding 'before signing the agreement, each spouse party was provided with independent legal advice from a legal practitioner about the effect of the agreement on the rights of that party and about the advantages and disadvantages, at the time that the advice was provided, to that party of making the agreement'.

Whether you are the party who is having the financial agreement prepared or the party who is receiving the agreement for advice, **it is imperative that you receive detailed advice** which covers the following:

- your obligations in entering into the agreement including your obligations for full disclosure
- the current law as set out in the Family Law Act as it relates to property settlement matters
- how the law might apply to you if you were to separate without the agreement in place either within a few years or a number of years and
- whether it is in your interests to enter into the agreement.

The requirement that both parties receive independent legal advice is fundamentally important where you are saying that you do not want the assistance of the court to determine your property settlement matter in the event that you separate. If you have entered into an agreement which is not favourable, then the Family Law Act requires that you receive proper advice about that.

After you have received this advice, you may be asked to sign a copy of the letter to confirm that you have read and received the required legal advice.

It is important that both parties to the agreement receive the same level of advice. It is not a simple process of one party seeing a lawyer to 'just sign off' on the advice. Both parties should make an assessment about the advice they are to receive. If one party does not receive sufficient advice, there is a risk that the agreement can be later set aside.

Signing the agreement

Once the advice has been given, then the lawyers are in a position to sign off on the agreement. This is usually done at the time the agreement is signed by the parties.

Again, the Family Law Act says: 'either before or after signing the agreement, each spouse party was provided with a signed statement by the legal practitioner stating that the advice [regarding the effect on your rights and the advantages and disadvantages] was provided to that party and 'either before or after signing the agreement, each spouse party was provided with a signed statement by the legal practitioner stating that the advice … was provided to that party'.

The same agreement must be signed by both parties, that is, the agreement cannot be signed in counter-parts with each party signing a separate document. In practice, one party signs with their lawyer and then the other party signs with their lawyer.

Finalising, exchanging and storing the agreement

After the agreement has been signed, one party or their lawyer should retain the original and the other party should retain a copy. Either way, both parties to the agreement should have a copy of the agreement. The original agreement should be stored in a safe location.

As can be seen from the above **there is a lot of work that goes into preparing a financial agreement** to ensure that the agreement is binding and the risks of having the agreement set aside by the court in the future are low.

Ready for the future

WHAT ARE ESTATE-PLANNING DOCUMENTS?

Estate-planning documents are legal documents that are used to outline how a person's assets and personal affairs will be managed in the event of their incapacity or death. Estate-planning documents can help ensure that a person's wishes are carried out and can provide peace of mind for themselves and their loved ones.

There are generally three main documents considered in an estate-planning context:

- a will (including testamentary trusts)
- an enduring power of attorney
- an advance health directive.

There are other documents of course including setting up trust structures which exist while you are alive and can continue after your death.

Broadly, here are some definitions of these important estate-planning documents.

Last will and testament: A last will and testament is a legal document that outlines how a person's assets will be distributed after their death. It can also be used to appoint guardians for minor children and to name an executor to manage the distribution of assets.

Enduring power of attorney: A power of attorney is a legal document that appoints a person to act on behalf of another person in financial and legal matters. A power of attorney can be used to manage a person's affairs if they become incapacitated or unable to make decisions.

Advance health directive: An advance health directive is a legal document that outlines a person's wishes for medical treatment in the event that they become incapacitated or unable to communicate their wishes.

WHAT IS A WILL AND WHY HAVE ONE

A will is a legal instrument which sets out who you leave your estate to. Your estate can include property you own, a house, investments, shares and personal property including jewellery and family heirlooms. Importantly your will also appoints a person who will sort everything out, close your accounts, transfer property, sell and distribute things. As you will see in this section, **if you don't have a will, then the law determines who is to administer your estate and how your estate is to be divided**. The more complex your family scenario the more complicated this distribution can be. The law does not take into account separation, only divorce. The law does not take into account your relationship with your family and whether they should receive a share of your estate.

A will allows you to determine who receives your estate and who will be responsible for sorting everything out. A will allows you to say who receives what property and how much they receive along with others. There are certain factors that you need to take into account which you will see below, however, you have the ability to put in your will whatever your wishes are.

I don't own any property so why do I need a will?

I quite often get asked this question and then when we dig deeper, we work out that the person quite often does own some form of property. But let's take a step back. There are, in my mind, two key reasons why you would have a will. The first is important and that is defining your beneficiaries and who will inherit your estate.

The second key reason, and one of the more important aspects to having a will, however, is the appointment of someone to assist in the running around and tidying up of your affairs.

Case Study

Charlotte's son Chris passed away before her. He was around forty years of age. At law, Charlotte was the first in line to be responsible for the administration of the estate. She needed to step in and finalise all of her son's affairs. The difficulty was that Chris didn't leave a will. He had a number of different superannuation company interests from working various jobs from time to time and he had otherwise acquired a lot of debt. Charlotte was the one tasked with sorting that out. Because Chris didn't have a will, it meant that each time Charlotte tried to speak to one of the entities, she had to prove who she was and why was authorised to take these steps.

If Chris had had a will which appointed either Charlotte or another person, then that person would be duly authorised to get on and assist and administer the estate. Where a person dies without a will, sometimes there is uncertainty about who may make an application or who is entitled to take those steps.

It was a modest estate and there was insufficient money to be able to apply for a grant of probate and so Charlotte did the best she could, writing to each of the entities to pull together the estate. It was a long process and each time Charlotte had to write those words in a letter, she was reminded that her son had passed away before her. It was quite a traumatic process.

It is for this reason that having a will who appoints a person to act as your **executor**, even when your estate is modest, is so very important. Giving a person authority so that they can get on and administer your estate without the distress that goes with proving who they are on each and every occasion removes significant stress and heartache from the process.

Returning then to the question of whether you have anything to give away at all – if you have had any sort of job, since you turned fifteen or whatever the legal age was when you were able to start to work, you will have some superannuation interests. There is likely a TPD (total permanent disability) or life policy attached to that superannuation. You might have a car; it might be a little old car but it's still a car nonetheless and somebody will have to deal with it when you've passed away.

Just because you don't have real estate or other investments and shares and those sorts of things doesn't mean having a will is not necessary. It is likely that you will own something of importance that you will want to give away. You want to make sure with some certainty who receives your book collection or your jewellery, your pet or your favourite couch. At the very least you'll want to give the superannuation company some direction about what happens with your super.

What happens without a will

If a person dies without a valid will this is described as dying 'intestate'. Each state and territory in Australia varies slightly and it is important to speak to a lawyer where you live for information about the law as it applies in your home town. Here we focus on the law in Queensland.

Part 3 of the Succession Act 1981 (the Act) in Queensland contains provisions for estate administration when someone dies intestate. Schedule 2 contains the details of what happens in different circumstances depending on whether there is a surviving spouse, child or other family. In the Act, children are referred to as issue.

If a person you are related to has died without a will, **it is best to consult with a lawyer for advice about how the estate is to be distributed and who has authority to administer the estate**. People who are relevant relations and may be able to administer the estate are any surviving spouse, children (issue), along with brothers and sisters, grandparents of the deceased as well as siblings of a parent of the deceased, and any children of any siblings of a parent of the deceased.

This distribution may not reflect your wishes or your family's needs, but there may not be anything they can do. Some people you consider family may also be excluded from the rules of distribution – for example, step-parents, mother/father in law, and relatives more remote than first cousins are all excluded from the provisions. Further, if there are children, a surviving spouse does not automatically receive the estate.

If you have no living relatives and die without a valid will, your estate is paid to the state government. A will would allow you to avoid this and perhaps donate your estate to a charity or a cause which you support.

SO HOW DOES THE ESTATE GET DISTRIBUTED THEN?

When a person dies without a will in Queensland, there are certain rules that determine who inherits the estate. It depends on whether the person who died had a spouse or children or neither and what other family there is.

If there is a spouse, but no children, then the spouse will receive the entire estate. If there is a spouse and children, then the spouse will receive the first $150,000 of value in the estate along with the household chattels, plus either one half or one third of what's left, depending on how many children there are. If there is one child, the spouse will receive half of the residuary. If there are two children or more, then the spouse will receive one third and the balance will be shared between the children.

If there is no spouse, then the children are the only beneficiaries. If there is no spouse and no children, then in this order, the following family members are entitled to the estate: parents, then brothers, sisters, nieces and nephews, then grandparents, then aunts, uncles, and cousins. If there are no family members at all, having regard to all of the people within a family tree, then the state is the beneficiary. That is the government receives the benefit of the estate.

At first glance, some consider the intestacy rules to be quite a straightforward distribution. For example, if they have a spouse and they have been in a relationship with that person for a period of time, then why complicate things, everything should go to the spouse anyway. Where things do get complicated is where there is no spouse or the definition of spouse is murky. You may have only been together for a short period of time. There might be a question over whether you are in a genuine de facto relationship. It's certainly different if you're married, regardless of how long you've been together. If you have children from a prior relationship, then that needs to be considered, and that may impact what ultimately happens to the distribution of your estate.

How does my estate get administered without a will?

If a person has died without a will, **someone will likely need to apply for letters of administration to administer the estate**. This document will provide the administrator with authority to deal with the estate. This will generally be required before financial institutions will release any assets from the estate.

The Supreme Court must be satisfied that the person applying is the appropriate person to apply. Priority is given in accordance with the court rules and is generally as follows: spouse, child, grandchild, parents, siblings and so on.

In order to obtain a grant of letters of administration your administrator must do the following:

- advertise their intention to apply for letters of administration. This involves placing an advertisement in the *Queensland Law Reporter*
- provide a copy of this advertisement to the public trustee
- after fourteen days has passed, file an application for letters of administration in the Supreme Court. Your administrator will need to file an affidavit confirming they are the appropriate person to apply, and one confirming that the advertising requirements have been met. Your administrator will also need to file the original death certificate; this will not be returned
- the court will then issue the grant of letters of administration, usually within six to eight weeks of the application being filed.

After you have obtained a grant of letters of administration, your administrator will then have the **formal authority** of the court to undertake the actions required to administer the estate.

Case Study

Jessica came to see us for advice regarding her mother's estate. Jessica was the eldest daughter. She had a brother Cameron and a half-brother Thomas. Jessica's mother, Bianca, died without a will. As the eldest daughter, Jessica sought to apply for letters of administration to administer her mother's estate. Jessica, along with Cameron and Thomas, would be the beneficiaries of the estate as they were the only children of Bianca.

As we worked through the administration of the estate and in particular the application for letters of administration, we ticked off the requirements in ruling out past potential applicants. In this case,

Bianca had previously been married on a number of occasions, but most recently she was married to Rodney. We asked Jessica to obtain a copy of the divorce certificate for the marriage between Bianca and Rodney, so that we could finalise the application for letters of administration. Jessica had the application for divorce. It had been signed and lodged with the court. She couldn't locate the divorce certificate. We emailed the Family Court registry to obtain a copy of the divorce certificate to attach to the application. The court emailed back; it seemed that the Bianca filed the application but didn't turn up to her divorce hearing. And on that basis, the court dismissed the divorce application and at law Bianca remained married to Rodney. They had been separated for nineteen years.

This meant that Rodney was legally Bianca's spouse. Despite having had a property settlement nineteen years ago, Rodney was entitled to a further distribution because Bianca did not have a will. To make matters worse, Rodney was the father of Thomas, though not the father of Jessica and Cameron. So there was a reasonable amount of animosity within the family.

While the matter for Jessica and her family was ultimately resolved, it was not without a significant legal expense, but also emotional angst. Jessica was stuck on a rollercoaster endeavouring to administer her mother's estate for eighteen months after her mother passed away. She could not let go of the dispute between the parties or take the time to grieve the loss of her mother, when she was engaged in a battle as such with her mother's ex-spouse and their son.

In the same way that divorce can have an impact on when you can remarry, separation and divorce have an impact on your will. Your spouse remains your spouse at law until the divorce order is granted. **Separation is not enough to end a spouse relationship when there has been a marriage.** It is different for a de facto relationship where the limitation period ends two years after separation.

For this reason, when parties separate, we encourage them to prepare a new will so that there can be no question of a potential distribution to a former spouse.

In the case study above, if Bianca had prepared a new will, then Jessica, Cameron and Thomas would have been saved this dispute and the estate would have been distributed in accordance with Bianca's wishes.

What are the practical consequences of not having a will?

As you can see, there is much uncertainty if you die without a will.

In summary:

- your estate may be distributed in a manner which you didn't contemplate or didn't wish for
- additional stress may be caused to your family, who will have to sort out your estate and may encounter conflict between the beneficiaries
- there could be possible additional costs for your family in making an application for letters of administration, particularly if your estate is straight forward.

What is involved in preparing a will

Hopefully now I have convinced you about the importance of having a will. Let's turn then to what is involved in preparing a will. Here we need to consider the following:

- who can prepare a will?
- who is involved when preparing your will?
- how do you distribute your property?
- what property is excluded from your will?
- how often should you review your will?

Who can prepare a will?

In order to prepare a will, you must have **testamentary capacity**. You must understand the nature of your will and know and approve the contents of your will. For example, do you know what property you have. Do you know who you are appointing within your will to be your executor. More broadly, do you know what year it is, where you are and why you want to prepare your will.

The legal definition of testamentary capacity is that the testator understands the nature of the act and its effects; they understand the extent of the property that they're giving away; they understand, comprehend and appreciate the claims which could potentially be made on the estate; and they are of sound mind.

Provided you have testamentary capacity you can prepare a will.

If you have lost capacity through age or for medical reasons such as dementia or Alzheimer's, then you are unable to prepare a will.

You must be over the age of eighteen years to prepare a will. In certain limited circumstances an application can be made to the court asking that a will be prepared for a person under the age of eighteen years. This is usually done in exceptional circumstances where the child is likely to die before the age of eighteen and has specific wishes.

In summary, generally so long as you are over the age of eighteen and understand your affairs, you can prepare a will.

Who is involved when preparing your will?

There are a number of different people involved when you prepare a will.

- **The testator** – this is you, the person who is preparing the will
- **Your executor** – this is the person who administers your estate
- **Your beneficiaries** – these are the people who will benefit from your estate
- **Guardians** – if you have children who are under the age of eighteen years, then you can nominate a guardian for any minor children.

The executor of your estate

The role of the executor is to ensure your wishes are followed and your estate is distributed in accordance with your will. Executors have certain duties when administering your estate, such as calling in all of your assets, settling certain debts and liabilities, lodging tax returns, liaising with financial institutions and superannuation trustees and distributing your estate according to your will.

Appointing the right person is important for a variety of reasons. You should consider the following issues when deciding who to name as your executor.

A question for the 'ages'

One important factor to consider is the age of your executor relative to your own age, and their potential longevity in that role. The choice will vary according to your stage of life. An executor must be over the age of eighteen years.

Willing and able

It is important to consider whether the person you appoint as your executor is both willing, and able, to carry out the task. Try also to consider other factors such as whether your proposed executor has decided to move overseas or has extreme work commitments. Think about their abilities, too. If you have a large, complicated estate with many and varied classes of assets and liabilities, appointing your twenty-something child as executor is probably not going to be realistic. The nature and size of your estate will be an important factor in considering whom you appoint.

Young adults

If you are younger and making a will, then you might consider appointing a parent or close relative as your executor. If you are partnered, then you might appoint your spouse, if that relationship is stable and likely to be long-term. Appointing a friend could be problematic long-term as friendship groups do tend to change over time.

The 'middle years'

Most people in long-term relationships appoint their spouse as executor during these years. Most first-time wills are written at this time and usually because people start to get some significant assets in their estate. Also, this is the age for having children and most parents want to provide for them should the worst happen. Otherwise, siblings are often appropriate to appoint. Sometimes one's parents are past the age where acting as executor is possible and taking on the role of executor could be distressing to the elderly in many circumstances.

Older people

If you appointed an executor in the 'middle years', then you probably appointed a contemporary. Consider whether that person, who is likely now also of 'advancing years', is still appropriate. Will-makers in the later stage of life often appoint adult children or other trusted relatives younger than themselves.

Other things to think about for executors

Think about the **number of executors** to be appointed. We always recommend appointing at least two executors, so that if something happens to your first named executor, you are not left without an executor. You might appoint your parents or the survivor of them. You might appoint your parents and then a sibling. You might appoint your spouse in the first instance, and then a sibling as the backup. Appointing a backup means that if something were to happen to your first named executor, your will remains valid, and you will have the time and opportunity to be able to change your will if you need to.

Also note that the more people who are involved, the more people have to sign documents and be involved in taking the steps to administer the estate. If you appoint three executors, then all three executors need to sign all documents associated with the administration of the estate. This would apply if they are selling property that you own – three signatures on a contract, three signatures on the transfer documents. If they are dealing with banks, then there are three signatures that are required on each bank form. I once assisted in an estate where all six children were appointed as executors. The practicalities involved in having documents signed six times are significant.

While you might want to appoint a group of people to be fair, think practically about where they are and who they are and the number of them before settling on who you appoint.

Another consideration when thinking about who is an appropriate executor is their **location**. With today's families traveling far and wide, you may have family members overseas or interstate. It is important to think about the location of the person that you want to appoint as your executor. There are a lot of in-person documents that need to be signed when you are an executor. Having a think about the practical considerations of who you are appointing is key to reducing the costs and effort associated with the administration of your estate.

Think also about the **disposition of the person you are appointing**. Are they likely to cope with the administrative tasks that are involved? Do you think they might be so overwhelmed by the task at hand that they won't be able to carry out the role effectively? Are they meticulous with paperwork and banking and therefore will be able to efficiently move through the steps that need to be taken with your estate?

What if there is no valid executor when you die?
If you do not have a validly appointed executor, for example if your executors have passed away before you or do not have the capacity to undertake the role as executor, then a person will need to apply to administer your will. They need to apply for what is called a **grant of letters of administration with the will**. This means that they're still carrying out the terms of your will, just that there is no valid executor appointed pursuant to the will.

In those circumstances, there are particular people who have a right to bring an application for a grant of letters of administration. The first person who can apply is a trustee who may have been appointed to look after the residuary of the estate. The **residuary** is what is left after any specific or special individual gifts. If there is no trustee, then the next person who can apply is a person who is beneficially entitled to any part of the residuary estate. For example, if you appoint your spouse pursuant to your will, but your spouse has predeceased you, and the remainder of your estate is to go your brother, because you do not have children, then your brother is the person who can apply to be the administrator of your estate.

Considering your beneficiaries

The next category of person to consider when preparing a will is your **beneficiaries**. Your beneficiaries are those who are to receive an inheritance pursuant to your will. You can leave your estate to whomever you wish. The law in Queensland, and elsewhere within Australia, provides that there are certain categories of beneficiary that you must consider when preparing your will. These categories of beneficiaries are those who have a right to bring a claim on your estate in the event that they have not received a benefit (adequate provision) from your estate.

The law requires that a testator gives more consideration to providing for their spouse, their children or another minor dependent, living with them at their death and being provided for at their death.

If you are determined not to make provision for a spouse or children, and there are reasons for you doing that, then it is important that you talk to your lawyer about this.

In addition to family members, you can also provide for requests to charities if there are certain institutions that you have been affiliated with during your lifetime that you wish to benefit. Your lawyer can talk to you about the wording of these particular clauses.

You can provide for your estate to be held on trust for minor beneficiaries until they turn certain ages in circumstances where a beneficiary must be eighteen years of age before they can receive the benefit to be paid to them.

Appointing a guardian to care for young children

The next category of person is a guardian for your children. If you have minor children, you can nominate a person who would act as the guardian for the children in the event that the remaining parent of that child or children had passed away before you. It is a good idea to have a talk to the people that you are considering appointing as guardian for any minor children that you have.

How do you distribute your property?

The reality is that you can distribute your estate however you wish (subject to a couple of excluded things we'll refer to below). If you own property by yourself or have money in the bank, you can leave these things to family, you can donate to a charity that you want to support, or you can leave your estate to friends or siblings. You can do whatever you wish.

However (and you knew there was a 'however' coming) … as mentioned above there are certain people whom you need to consider when making your will. These people are those who might be able to make a claim on your estate if they feel they haven't been adequately provided for.

The law allows certain people to bring a claim for further provision from an estate where they have not received adequate provision to cover their needs. The law relating to estate claims is far more involved than what we will cover in this book. It is important to understand these key points:

- certain people have a right to bring a claim against an estate for further provision if they haven't had adequate provision to provide for their needs
- those people are a person's spouse and their children
- there is a third category of person who can bring a claim against an estate called a 'dependant'. A dependant is a person being wholly or substantially maintained by the deceased person at

their death who is a parent of the deceased, a parent of a surviving child who is under eighteen or a person under eighteen.

Just because a right exists for a person to bring a claim on the estate does not mean they will be successful.

The **financial circumstances** of the person bringing the claim is extremely relevant where they must prove that they have a need for further provision.

The **relationship** between the deceased person and the claimant is key and issues of poor behaviour, disentitling conduct and estrangement are to be considered.

So what do you do with all of this information? While you can leave your estate however you please, you must have given consideration to whom you are leaving your estate to and if you choose to exclude a spouse, child or dependant, talk to your lawyer about why. You might consider preparing a statement of wishes setting out why you have made the decisions you have made.

What property is excluded from your will?

There are a couple of items of property which are excluded from your will. These are items which you cannot give away under your will. You may be able to provide some directions about what is to happen, however unless they form part of your estate, you cannot direct where they are to go.

The property we will consider here is:

- superannuation
- jointly owned property
- trusts.

The funny thing about superannuation

When we talk about this topic at our regular webinars and workshops, most are surprised to know that you can't give your superannuation away under your will. In fact you can't do much with your superannuation unless you have some particular documents in place. While superannuation is an asset that you have, that your employer contributes to over the years of working, at the end of the day, **it is the trustee of your superannuation fund that ultimately determines how your superannuation will be paid**. Your superannuation trustee has absolute discretion about the payment of your superannuation. You cannot gift your superannuation in your will.

If you have a standard industry fund or other private superannuation fund, then the trustee of that fund manages and controls what happens to your superannuation interest. If you have a self-managed superannuation fund, then it is likely that your superannuation will be paid as you want it to be paid and we'll come to this shortly.

When you complete the forms on your superannuation fund, you are always given the option to **nominate beneficiaries** for your account. You will go through and complete the form for the setup of the fund, and you will type in the beneficiaries of the account such as your parents or your children or your spouse. You will then continue on and tick some more boxes and set up your fund. What you have created is a simple nomination. It's something that your trustee of your superannuation fund takes into account when determining where to pay your superannuation but it's in no way binding.

The alternative is to enter into what is known as a **binding death benefit nomination**. A binding nomination, as the name suggests, binds the trustee of your superannuation fund to pay your superannuation as directed. It is different to the standard nomination you complete when you fill out your application for super. You will know if you have completed a binding nomination if you have obtained a form, printed a form, filled it out and signed it in the presence of two witnesses. Preparing a binding death benefit nomination requires the same process as if you were signing your will.

If you are not sure about whether you have completed this process, you can usually Google the name of your superannuation fund and 'binding death benefit nomination form' to locate the form for your particular fund. Have a look at the fund form, see whether you've completed it and if not, you can always ring the fund to find out. Since the process involves you completing a paper form with two witnesses, it is likely to be something that you will remember doing. Remember it is different to simply ticking a box and filling out the online form when you open or update your super fund.

A **binding death benefit nomination form** allows you to specify who your superannuation is to be paid to.

You can pay your superannuation to a spouse, to children or to a friend. You can even pay your superannuation to your estate. There are different tax consequences depending upon the type of beneficiary that you nominate to pay your superannuation to. That sort of tax advice is financial advice and it goes beyond the scope of what we can tell you about in this book. The most we can say is that where your superannuation is paid to a dependent such as a spouse or a child under the age of eighteen then the tax consequences are less than if the superannuation is paid to a non-dependent.

How you fill out your binding death benefit nomination form requires a combination of legal advice and financial advice for these reasons. Your lawyer can let you know what the options are and there might be some strategy involved in paying your superannuation to a spouse or to the estate or directly to children depending on your individual circumstances.

Coming back to self-managed superannuation funds, in the setup of a self-managed superannuation fund ordinarily there is a binding nomination included in the set-up documents which provides for the fund to be paid to the remaining spouse within the fund. You should check the set-up documents if you have a self-managed superannuation fund to check if this applies to your fund. You can also ask the accountant or financial advisor who assisted you to set up the fund.

What about joint property?

Firstly it is important to understand what is joint property and when we talk about property we need to consider whether we are referring to your home, investment real estate, or other things that you own.

Let's talk about the word property first. From a lawyer perspective, **'property' is all inclusive**; it includes 'real property' such as houses, land or apartments; it also includes 'personal property' such as superannuation, bank accounts, jewellery, shares, furniture, antiques, collectables and other items which are personal. Regardless of whether you have personal property or real property – property can be owned jointly, that is with another person or persons or solely, that is on your own.

Real property has one further distinction when it is owned jointly. You can own your house or unit either as joint tenants or tenants in common.

Upon death, joint property, whether real or personal, will automatically be transferred to the survivor. If you own joint share holdings, a joint bank account, real property as **joint tenants**, the property will automatically transfer to the surviving owner on death.

If you have, for example, jointly owned property, you might own property jointly with a spouse. Then as a joint tenancy, the survivor of that property will be the person who automatically receives it. Most of the time when you buy property, you will own it jointly unless you've specifically given your conveyancing solicitor some instructions to hold it differently. You can hold it as joint tenants or the other way to hold properties is as **tenants in common**, which it's still technically joint property, but you own two separate and distinct shares as opposed to one share together. If you own property as a joint tenant, it will automatically go to the survivor. The same applies with joint bank accounts or joint shareholdings, and those sorts of things. If one of you passes away, automatically, the rest is going to go to the survivor. If you own property as tenants in common you own separate shares and your share will pass to your named beneficiary in your will.

Family trusts

Trusts are instruments created to hold property or undertake business. When property is owned by a trust, it is held separately to your will. In essence it sits within its own trust and as such you are **unable to gift it under your will**.

It is important that you seek advice from a lawyer or an accountant about any structures that you have set up. When setting up a business, some people create trusts and companies without necessarily appreciating the impact that the structure will have on their estate plan. While you can provide direction about certain aspects of the property you own in a trust, ultimately the power for the distribution of those trust assets will rest with your trustee.

You're also not entitled to give away money which might be held by your family trust or discretionary trust, or if you're the sole director of a company, because they're separate and distinct legal entities so they do not fall inside your will. So if you have property which is held inside a family trust, even though you might be the beneficiary of that family trust, you're not entitled to give away that property while it remains within the family trust.

What is a testamentary trust and do I need one?

In a trust, one person (the trustee) is given the responsibility of managing assets for the benefit of another person or people (the beneficiaries). A testamentary trust is a type of trust that is established through a person's will and comes into effect after the person's death. Unlike a family or other discretionary trusts, which are established during a person's lifetime, a testamentary trust is created through a will and only goes into effect after the person has passed away.

The will sets out the terms of the testamentary trust. The assets are placed into the trust, and a trustee is appointed to manage the trust and distribute the assets according to the terms of the trust. The trust may impose limitations on some or all beneficiaries, or alternatively, they may provide them a great deal of control.

Typically, testamentary trusts are discretionary trusts, meaning that the trustee is free to choose how to distribute the assets among the beneficiaries.

There are a **number of reasons why a testamentary trust might be the right estate-planning model for you**.

A testamentary trust can provide you more influence over how your assets are allocated after your passing, which is one of its advantages. For instance, you can choose that the assets be given to your beneficiaries gradually rather than all at once, or that the assets be used to pay for particular costs like schooling or health care.

Testamentary trusts can also ensure that the bequest is distributed to the correct parties. An independent trustee can ensure that beneficiaries who are at risk, such as small children or the sick, unable or disabled, will be taken care of.

If the beneficiaries might be susceptible to litigation or bankruptcy, such as individuals who work in high-risk industries or professions, testamentary trusts are also a sensible precaution.

Additionally, trusts can, when prepared properly, prevent the effects of divorce and ensure that assets will be left to the testator's children or grandchildren in the event of divorce or a subsequent marriage.

There are also tax advantages. A major benefit of testamentary trusts is that they enable the beneficiaries to receive any benefit in the most tax-effective manner possible. Trusts allowing for income splitting ensure that benefits are distributed where possible at lower tax rates depending on the type of beneficiary.

Before deciding if a testamentary trust is necessary, it's a good idea to consult with an experienced estate-planning lawyer. A lawyer can help you understand the potential advantages and disadvantages of setting up a trust and can offer essential advice on whether a testamentary trust is appropriate for your particular situation.

A lawyer can also assist you in comprehending the needs for establishing and preserving a testamentary trust, as well as the legal and tax ramifications of doing so. A testamentary trust, for instance, must be mentioned in the testator's will and must abide by all applicable local, state and federal laws and regulations.

Additionally, a lawyer can assist you in deciding if a testamentary trust is the right option for your estate-planning requirements. A family trust or other estate-planning tools may be more suitable depending on your particular situation.

What is an enduring power of attorney?

An enduring power of attorney involves preparing a document authorising a person to make decisions and take actions in relation to personal or financial matters on your behalf **if you lose the capacity** to make these decisions for yourself.

The power to make decisions over personal matters will only come into effect if you lose the capability to make such decisions. Personal matters include health matters but doesn't extend to special personal matters or special health matters.

The power to make financial decisions can come into effect whenever you choose.

Who should you appoint as your attorney?

This person can be a friend or relative or a professional person. The decision should be made carefully as their decisions will have the same legal power as decisions you make about yourself. You can appoint more than one person. **You should appoint someone you trust.**

Important things to note

While enduring powers of attorney are important for the elderly, it is also a good way to protect yourself and your loved ones in case something happens as part of your broader estate plan.

There are different circumstances that can lead to loss of capacity – such as an acquired brain injury, the on-set of dementia or a temporary illness or condition such as delirium.

While these are unlikely and unpleasant to think about, if you have prepared an enduring power of attorney document then in the unlikely case of such a situation, your partner or loved ones will be empowered to act in your best wishes. If you are over eighteen, you should make an enduring power of attorney. You could do this at the same time you organise your will.

Requirements for giving enduring power of attorney

To prepare an enduring power of attorney, you must have the capacity to make an enduring document. This includes understanding the nature and effect of the power and in particular this includes understanding the following:

- that you can limit the power and instruct the attorney about how to exercise the power
- when the power begins
- that once the power begins the attorney has power and full control over the matter, subject to the terms
- the power can be revoked
- the power continues if the principal becomes a person with impaired capacity
- if the principal is not capable of revoking the power, they cannot effectively oversee the use of the power either.

Enduring power of attorney document

To be a valid enduring power of attorney, the document must:

- be in the approved form
- be signed by the principal
- be signed and dated by an eligible witness.

How often should I review my enduring power of attorney?

We recommend that you review your documents regularly and consult with a lawyer if you wish to change them, especially if any of the following events occur:

- you change your name or anyone named in the enduring power of attorney changes their name
- if an attorney dies or becomes unwilling or unsuitable to act due to ill-health, age or for any other reason
- if the family situation of you or any attorney changes (e.g. marriage, divorce, matrimonial problems, children or further children, de facto relationship)

- if you become involved in a new business, company or trust and
- if you take up permanent residence in another state or overseas.

Do you need an advance health directive?

If you consider your three estate-planning documents in this way, your enduring power of attorney is a document used when you lose capacity or are losing capacity and decisions need to be made on your behalf. Your will is read once you die. Your advance health directive is the document in between. **This document sets out your directions for how the end of your life is to be managed.**

The advanced health directive is a document completed in two parts. The first relates to medical questions that are ordinarily completed with the assistance of your general practitioner. Your general practitioner needs to sign a certificate confirming that you understand the nature and effect of the document you are signing when you give instructions about the end of your life.

The second part of the document relates to the legal advice required to be received. Again you are making a document that dictates what steps are to be taken at the end of your life including medical treatment, if any.

You must receive legal advice about the nature and effect of the decisions you have made and a lawyer, justice of the peace or commissioner for declarations must certify that you understand the nature and effect of the document you are signing.

LIFE HAPPENS – WHEN TO REVIEW YOUR ESTATE PLAN

As lawyers we always impress upon our clients the importance of planning for the best but preparing for the worst. You've listened to the advice, done the right thing and made your will – so that's the end of it, right? Well, maybe not ... There are certain life events that may have an impact on your will which might necessitate another trip to the lawyer's office.

Getting married? Time to check your will and may need a new one ...

Planning a wedding is a wonderful, exciting time full of fun and plenty of stress, with many important decisions to make. It's a time to celebrate love and life, so not many people want to turn their minds to dying when they think about getting married. Generally, you are kept busy making arrangements, meeting with vendors and suppliers and all that other stuff that goes along with planning a wedding. Making or revising your will is likely to be very low on the priorities list in the lead up to the big day.

It might be that you have been together many years, had children, built assets and for all intents and purposes, lived the life of a married couple for some time. You may have made wills early on and never really given it much more thought since.

The reason to consider your current will or to make a new will is that in Queensland, **getting married automatically revokes your existing will**. There are some exceptions which provide that if the person you appoint as your executor or the person you give your estate to is also the person you are marrying, then the clauses which make those appointments or give those gifts are not revoked. So, it's important to see your lawyer to either check that your current will is okay or prepare a new will.

It is not necessary, or indeed desirable, to wait until after you get married to get this done. We can use a simple drafting technique to include a clause stating that the will is made in contemplation of your upcoming marriage. This means you can make your new will in contemplation of your wedding before the wedding day. That way you don't run the risk of dying intestate (without a will) because you never got around to making that appointment. It's also the perfect opportunity to tweak any parts of your will that no longer fit your current circumstances.

Ending a relationship? You really need a will!

Consider the strange state of affairs that can arise when a couple decide to go their separate ways. While some people move on and start new lives upon separation, the formal divorce order takes some time. This is important as **it is the divorce order that formally ends a marriage**.

To obtain a divorce order the parties must be separated for at least twelve months. Then a divorce application might take two to three months to be heard. And then the divorce order issues one month and one day after that. On average, from the date of separation, if you lodge your application as soon as the twelve months rolls around, it's about fifteen to sixteen months between separation and divorce order. So what happens if, between the breakdown of the relationship and the divorce being granted, one of the parties dies without leaving a will?

The strange answer is that the surviving estranged spouse may be entitled to take most, if not all (depending on the circumstances), of the deceased spouse's property. This will even be the case where the spouses have consent orders filed in the Family Law Courts and duly sealed to divide the property of the marriage. Go back to page 75 and read the curious case of Bianca, who had separated from Rodney some nineteen years earlier but did not turn up to the divorce hearing, leaving Rodney as her primary beneficiary. The lesson to be learnt here: if you separate from your spouse, see your solicitor immediately and prepare a new will!

Getting divorced? Some of your will is automatically revoked

Once your divorce has been granted **any mention of your former spouse in your will (whether as executor or beneficiary) is automatically revoked**. All other terms in your will remain valid. Depending on the drafting of the will, this will usually mean the gift either goes to the former spouse's children, or to the person who gets the balance of the estate, or 'residual beneficiary'. Of course, the will can be drafted in such a way that the operation of this section is avoided, if that's what the testator wants.

Noting though that it can take fifteen to sixteen months for a divorce order to come through, it's usually not worth the wait and changing your will at separation is the most prudent course.

Something happens to one of your executors or beneficiaries

A well-drafted will should deal with contingencies such as an executor or beneficiary named in your will predeceasing you.

Your executor may not be able to act on behalf of your estate when the time comes around. They may have died before you. They may be older and unable to take up the role of executor. There may be a question of whether they have capacity to act and administer the estate.

In those circumstances it is recommended that at the time of drafting your will, you consider appointing an appropriate executor and a backup. Think about those things referred to earlier in this book about the age and disposition of the executor when you appoint them. While you won't have a crystal ball available to consider all possible outcomes, you will be able to think through what would happen if something happened to your first choice.

The same applies with beneficiaries. At the beginning of your relationship, you may not yet have children or have even contemplated children. This does not stop you from providing for children in the future. In a new relationship for example, where you are getting married or starting out a long-term de facto relationship, you might think about a will that covers the following:

- providing for your spouse to be your primary beneficiary
- if your spouse dies before you, providing for any children you may have. This means you don't have to redraft your will if you haven't included children and later have children.
- if you don't end up having children, providing for your siblings or other beneficiaries as the case may be.

Thinking about your will this way means that you can go on with your relationship and not worry about having to change things if you have children. If you had instead prepared a will which said the following, things might be different:

- providing for your spouse to be your primary beneficiary
- if your spouse dies before you, providing for your estate to go to your siblings – perhaps half to your siblings and half to the siblings of your spouse.
- if you subsequently had children, you would need to change your will. If you didn't change your will and your spouse died before you then you have not provided for your children. Your children would then fall into that category of people who would bring a claim on your estate, causing costs and no doubt distress to all involved.

When we prepare wills, we try to consider as many outcomes as possible to assist you to work through different scenarios. We can't always provide for all eventualities, but we can assist in talking through what might be possible.

The best course of action is to be sure that firstly, you have a will, and secondly, keep in mind the impact of certain life events on that will. **You will probably need to change, replace or update your will over time.** Try not to put it off because the consequences to your loved ones can be significant.

Empowered by information

THE IMPORTANCE OF INFORMATION AND KNOWLEDGE

There is power in knowledge. The more you know, the better you can make decisions about matters that impact your life. In my book *Trust Yourself: How Empowered Decision Making Will Help You Resolve Your Family Law Matter* I call this **empowered decision-making –** that is, if you know the law, the system, your matter, the reality and how those variables align with your goals, you will have the power to make decisions that produce the outcomes you are trying to achieve.

In that book, I posed the question in the context of separation – if you were offered the opportunity to determine your family law outcome by being equipped with a deep understanding of your facts, the law, the system, the reality and your goals, would you take it? A process that empowers you to make critical decisions, resolve your family law matter and get on with your life surely is appealing.

The same can be said in a pre-separation and pre-relationship world.

The more information you have, the better you can make more informed decisions. Knowledge empowers you to make the right decisions for you.

While we don't all have a crystal ball to tell us what the future holds, if you can make the right decisions early on and have sensible conversations about how things will work, you can endeavour to avoid possible heartache down the track. And while your heart may be broken at some point, if those conversations have been had, you will likely find yourself coming out the other end in a much better space.

The law touches every person throughout their days, weeks and lives without many being aware or having reason to question it. From the transaction to purchase a new car (signing a contract) to buying a new surfboard (sale of goods), moving into a new property (contract or tenancy agreement), or having a lovely meal out (food and licensing requirements), daily life goes on without much need to think about these legal transactions.

The law is generally only considered when things go wrong, when a dispute occurs or when you start planning your future. By this time, you might find it is too late, you are in more trouble than you thought, or things are messier or more out of order than they need to be. Generally, though, most people get by without considering the law or talking to a lawyer.

When you start a relationship though, some legal concepts are essential to understand so that you can move forward with knowledge and, ultimately, peace of mind knowing what you need to know.

And besides, with the (what some might term boring) legal bits out of the way, or at least considered and actioned, you can get on with living your life and enjoying your relationship because that, after all, is the ultimate goal.

THIS BOOK IS A START

It can be wonderful and exciting to begin a new relationship. It increases the likelihood that we may meet a spouse who shares our interests, values and passions. But starting a new relationship can also have challenges, and getting help and advice from others can help us work through those difficulties. Here are some reasons why it's beneficial to get assistance when beginning a new relationship.

Gain an outside perspective

It can be challenging to maintain objectivity and composure while we are in the throes of a new relationship. We can gain an objective viewpoint and see the relationship from a fresh perspective by asking friends, relatives or a counsellor for guidance. An outside view might help bring clarity since sometimes we may be too emotionally committed to the relationship to notice any red flags or warning signs.

Learn from others' experiences

Although it may seem like we are the only ones dealing with the difficulties of a new relationship, millions of other people have had similar experiences. We can learn from the successes and mistakes of others by asking for guidance, and then we can apply those lessons to our own relationships. Making decisions about our relationship based on the experiences of others might give us valuable insight into what works and what doesn't in a relationship.

Improve communication skills

Communication must be honest and efficient for a relationship to be healthy. We can develop better communication skills and learn how to express our emotions and concerns by asking for assistance. For instance, when we seek counsel from a qualified counsellor, they can teach us communication skills that we can apply to handle challenging interactions with our partner.

Reduce anxiety and stress

A new relationship's beginnings can be challenging and anxiety-inducing. By giving us direction and techniques to control our emotions, seeking advice might help ease some of that anxiety. Talking to friends or a therapist can help us feel less alone and isolated by providing us with a safe place to vent our worries and concerns.

Avoid common mistakes

Starting a new relationship may be both thrilling and overwhelming. We could make common mistakes that eventually harm the relationship.

We can steer clear of some of these typical mistakes and decide on our partnership in an informed manner by asking for assistance. For instance, at the beginning of a relationship, it's typical to move too rapidly and ignore crucial red flags. We can identify these pitfalls and take the appropriate precautions to prevent them by seeking guidance.

TALK TO EACH OTHER AND OTHER HELPFUL PEOPLE

Overall, open and honest communication is critical to building a solid and healthy relationship. Take the time to discuss these essential topics to establish a foundation of trust and understanding.

There is a range of topics to discuss, and managing your finances is one of the most significant conversations you will have.

Finances: It is crucial to discuss how you will manage your finances. How this conversation progresses may depend upon what stage of your life you are when you start your relationship.

If all is new and you are yet to acquire significant assets or wealth, then you may start on the journey with joint accounts and a joint venture. Suppose you are later in life or are coming into a relationship with significant wealth or have experienced a financial separation previously. In that case, you may be more cautious about joining joint accounts.

These are significant conversations to be had at the beginning of your relationship. I recently met a client who had lived her life with one account being the account in her husband's name. She can't recall quite how it happened but says that after about a year of being together, having worked full-time and successfully as a project manager until their marriage, her wages started to be paid into her husband's account. At the time, she thought this was probably normal. However, after thirty years of marriage, she can now see that it was one of the first stages of control by the husband. The husband controlled everything. Everything ended up in the husband's name.

Of course, we can never predict these things when we start in relationships. We hope for the best when we fall head over heels in love and accept this is how it is. Sometimes we don't know any better. The conversations we have in 2023 are very different from those had in the 1960s, 1970s and 1980s.

Having open and honest conversations about our expectations regarding money and accounts at the outset of a relationship provides a solid foundation for how those parts of our relationship will be managed in the future.

Other equally important topics include:

Relationship goals and plans: It's essential to discuss what you both want out of the relationship. Do you want something casual or serious? Are you looking for a long-term commitment? Discuss your future plans, including career goals, travel, and family. These conversations help you understand each other's priorities and ensure you're on the same page. Take, for example, the decision of whether to have children. One person may not wish to have children and the other may feel they are okay with that, but talking about it is important. Thinking that things are okay when they are not okay can leave one party feeling guilty and the other resentful.

Your communication style: Everyone communicates differently, so discussing your communication styles and preferences is important. Do you prefer to talk things out immediately or take time to process them first? Are there any off-limits topics?

Past relationships: Discussing past relationships can help you better understand each other. Conversations about your past are critical if your ex is still around as a co-parent, work colleague or friend. Be open and honest about your past relationships and any lessons you've learned.

Boundaries and expectations: Setting boundaries is vital in any relationship. Discuss what you're comfortable with and what you're not, and respect each other's boundaries. Talking about your expectations is particularly important to avoid arguments later. There is little point in grumbling when a particular chore isn't completed or communication is lacking if you have yet to make clear what you expect. Expectations are also important when considering things you want to continue to do in the relationship. If your commitment to the gym and fitness is vital, ensure that is known. If catching up with mates and fishing regularly is important, then talk about that.

Values and beliefs: Sharing your values and beliefs can help you understand each other better and ensure that you're compatible in the long term. If attending church is important to you, then be clear about that. If your partner is not religious, consider whether this will impact your relationship – will you be okay with heading to church on your own?

Family and friends: Discussing your relationships with family and friends can help you both understand each other's support systems. Understanding the dynamics in your family can ensure that awkward family situations are less likely to occur.

Intimacy: Communication about intimacy is essential to ensure both partners feel comfortable and respected. Discuss your boundaries, preferences and expectations.

You should consider a relationship counsellor if you need assistance talking to each other about these important concepts. Don't think of this in the traditional sense of 'couples therapy' but more so the ability to discuss your relationship foundations in a facilitated manner.

UNDERSTAND THE NUMBERS

When you are considering your estate plan or a pre-relationship advice, you should talk to a financial advisor or accountant, particularly if you are not sure what property you have or if you aren't quite sure how to deal with any property that you receive.

To lay a solid financial basis for your new relationship, it's crucial to have honest conversations regarding money. Working towards shared financial objectives and being open and honest about your finances can help avoid problems and foster trust.

If you are unable to talk about these things together, a financial advisor or accountant can help you to work through some of the following:

- **Income and expenses:** Discuss your individual incomes, expenses and financial obligations, such as debt and monthly bills. This can help you both understand each other's financial situation and plan accordingly.
- **Budgeting and saving:** Discuss your individual budgeting and saving habits and goals, and establish a joint budget and savings plan that works for both of you. This can help you both work towards shared financial goals and avoid conflicts over money.
- **Debt:** Discuss any debt that either partner has and how you plan to handle it. Will you tackle it together or separately? What strategies will you use to pay it off?
- **Joint or separate finances:** Discuss whether you want to keep your finances separate or merge them. This can depend on your individual financial goals and preferences.
- **Financial responsibilities:** Discuss how you will split financial responsibilities, such as paying bills or managing investments. Will one partner take on more financial responsibilities than the other?

- **Financial goals:** Discuss your shared financial goals, such as saving for a down payment on a house or retirement and make a plan to work towards them together.
- **Your entities and any necessary tax advice:** Discuss what you have, how they will be managed, whether those entities are necessary or the best vehicle for what you are trying to achieve.

LAWYERS ARE HELPFUL PEOPLE

How do you choose the right lawyer for you?

Working through your personal legal affairs, whether that is the preparation of a will or considering a prenuptial agreement is a profoundly personal journey. The person you choose to guide you through the process is therefore a significant decision personal to you.

Over the years I have asked my clients about the important things they looked for when choosing their lawyer. Their responses vary, but key themes do emerge; while some of these themes won't apply to everyone, they do offer some points to consider.

Case study

Stephanie came to see me in a state of high stress and anxiety. She had been in a relationship for three years, had two very young children and was parenting her stepson on a full-time basis. The nature of Stephanie's relationship meant that when her ex-partner said 'jump', she said 'how high'. She had lived a life of walking on eggshells and was reactive to every demand that came. On reflection, Stephanie said:

'Before settling on my family lawyer, I had a meeting with another firm to discuss my legal issues. I came out of that meeting in tears, feeling very distressed and overwhelmed. My sister encouraged me to try again and to get a second opinion.

'Within minutes of meeting with my family lawyer, I felt safe. I suppose that is a strange word to use. But it was like a security blanket that I could trust I was being looked after. I almost immediately felt a gentle and kind approach, but with a confidence and strength that just made me feel completely safe and supported. For the first time since my legal issues had arisen, I felt that someone was taking my burden off my shoulders and allowing me to breathe for a moment. I came out of that first meeting smiling for the first time in a long time.'

While Stephanie's experience is important in the context of a family law separation, the themes are still relevant at the beginning of your relationship. You want that feeling of safety, of security, of knowing that your lawyer knows you, knows what you want to achieve and can help you get there. You want to feel confidence in your lawyer.

Here are some key points in considering which lawyer to choose:

A **personal referral** from a friend or other professional can be important. Through that referral you can understand that the lawyer has had an impact on the referrer such that they would gladly recommend their services. A professional referral could come from another lawyer or advisor and will generally be someone who has worked with the lawyer before. Lawyers stake a lot on their personal reputation and a personal referral is often the best endorsement a lawyer can have.

Their **core values must be aligned with your values**. There are many different tried and tested styles of legal practice when it comes to the personal nature of estate planning or family law. But you may not be looking for a robust, heavy-hitting lawyer who may lead you to victory at the cost of your relationships. Often greater success is had trying to work amicably or collaboratively, particularly where children are concerned.

One of my clients, Michelle said, 'I was looking for a lawyer who could handle but not unduly provoke the personality of my ex.'

Another client Craig said, 'I wanted to feel secure that my lawyer could deal with the psychology of the other party.'

Trust and confidence are crucial. These can only be established through meeting with your intended lawyer and developing a relationship based on the trust that they have the requisite experience to fully advise you in your circumstances and confidence that they can progress you to a resolution. My client Michelle said, 'The inability to make eye contact with me' was something that ruled out prior lawyers she had met with.

The ability to provide a **sense of calm or solidarity** in a chaotic or complex environment is key. Your family lawyer should talk through all of your anxieties and concerns and provide you with objective advice. This process has the ability to calm things down and assist clients with focusing on the big picture.

Your lawyer needs to truly **understand how you function as a person** and how you will respond to certain things. It is important to find someone who can advise you without talking down to you or patronising you, as well as being able to talk things through rather than just telling you how it is. While your lawyer can advise you on the law and the best approach, there must be give and take so that you can work together towards the goals that you have set. Having a lawyer who can manage that and work with you as a team is enormously beneficial.

A final key factor is to ensure that the lawyer you engage with has **a strong practice in the area in which you need advice**. If you have complicated property and structures and wish to set up the appropriate estate plan, see a lawyer who practices in that area. If you are looking for advice regarding a financial agreement (prenup), see a lawyer who has knowledge and expertise in family law. Take the time to find the lawyer who will be able to assist you. It is likely that your commercial lawyer who deals with your building or contract disputes will not be the best person to give you advice about your will or financial agreement.

As you can see from this list, it might take a couple of tries to find the right fit, and that's okay. Just because you have been to see a lawyer doesn't mean you are committed to that lawyer and are unable to change.

Preparing for your first visit to your lawyer

Regardless of what is important to you in selecting a lawyer who is right for you, it's important to prepare for your first appointment. In my years of practise, I have perceived a consistent pattern that those clients who take the time to think about what they want to achieve from their first meeting find the process more beneficial. While it is inevitable that some clients will not know where to start, usually due to the manner in which their relationship ended, most clients have the means to think through those things which are important to understand from this first meeting.

In particular I have found that by giving some attention to the following points in preparation, you will get the most out of your first visit to your lawyer.

Think about what property you have

Before seeking advice about your estate plan or family law relationship advice (e.g. prenuptial agreement), it is helpful for both you, and your lawyer in turn, if you sit down and work out what property you have and the value you anticipate each item of property has.

Your property might include your home and investment properties (whether you own these properties yourself, with someone else, or as part of a company or family trust). It also might include vehicles, money in the bank, shares and other investments, the contents in your home, and any companies or family trust structures. Property also includes any debt attached to any asset, such as a mortgage or margin lending loan, along with personal loans. Superannuation is also included as property, whether held in a normal fund or self-managed fund.

It is helpful if you can collect documents that show the value of the property that you have, such as recent bank statements, property valuations or superannuation statements.

You may need to talk to a financial advisor or accountant about what you have, particularly if you're not sure. Sometimes one person in the relationship knows all the financial information and the other person doesn't, and that's okay. Just pull together what you can.

Think about what you want to achieve to resolve your matter before your appointment, and take time to write down any questions that you might have

While the outcome in your matter will likely be determined by applying the law relevant to your circumstances, it is still very important to consider your goals – the outcomes that you want to achieve in resolving your matter. These may change after you have received advice about outcomes but setting goals prior to your first legal appointment will give you a clear direction to know where you are heading.

Think about the main questions you want to ask the lawyer. It is likely that you will have lots of questions and worries swirling around in your mind. Writing them down can help focus you on the important issues. A list of questions will also help your lawyer give you advice about those things which are concerning you, along with other advice you might need.

Come with an open mind

You will likely come across friends and family who have had to deal with similar legal matters to you, particularly in personal law matters such as estate planning and family law. While it is important to be supported by friends and family through any dispute that you might be facing, remember that your matter is different from anyone else's. Your family and circumstances surrounding your family are unique to you. There is no one-size-fits-all advice.

It may also be the case that your friends and family, as well-meaning as they might be, do not have all the information or legal knowledge to give you proper advice about your matter. It is not the case that you shouldn't listen to your friends and accept their support – simply be aware that unless they are lawyers, practising in the field in which you are experiencing problems, that the advice they give you might not be right for you.

Conclusion

Navigating a new relationship can be exciting and fulfilling. Still, it's essential to understand the legal and financial implications of the relationship to ensure that both partners are protected, and their interests are being met. Here are some key takeaways:

Firstly, it's important to understand when a relationship exists at law, particularly in common law relationships or de facto relationships. By understanding the legal definition of a relationship, both partners can ensure that their legal and financial rights are protected and that they are eligible for any benefits or entitlements that may be available to them.

Secondly, managing children and stepchildren in a new relationship can be challenging, and it's essential to be sensible and considerate in managing these relationships. Both partners can create a healthy and supportive family environment by prioritising open communication and fostering positive relationships with children and stepchildren.

Thirdly, financial planning is essential for any new relationship. By discussing financial goals, creating a budget and considering investments and retirement planning, partners can work together towards shared goals and ensure their financial needs and objectives are met.

Fourthly, having an estate plan is vital for ensuring that assets are distributed according to the individual's wishes and that loved ones are provided for in the event of death. By establishing a will or trust, both partners can ensure that their assets are managed and distributed in accordance with their wishes.

Finally, seeking advice from lawyers and counsellors can be incredibly beneficial for navigating a new relationship's legal and emotional complexities. Lawyers can provide legal advice and guidance on prenuptial agreements, estate planning and property ownership. Counsellors can provide emotional support and guidance for managing the challenges and opportunities of building a healthy and fulfilling relationship.

In summary, a new relationship can be a wonderful and rewarding experience, but it's crucial to approach it with caution and care. By understanding the legal and financial implications of the relationship, managing children and stepchildren effectively, engaging in financial planning, having an estate plan and seeking advice from professionals, both partners can create a healthy and fulfilling relationship that lasts a lifetime.

Acknowledgments

This book has been a long time in the making with the original concept starting in 2016. I put it aside for some time and focussed my efforts on what became my first book *Trust Yourself: How Empowered Decision Making Will Help You Resolve Your Family Law Matter*. A few years ago my sister-in-law **Tasha** said "so how is that next book coming along" and I was spurred into action again. So, thank you for the prod Tasha and here it is.

- To my friend **Ann** a special thank you – I'm grateful that in addition to being my publisher you are my book loving friend supporting me on my author journey. If you have a book to publish or a book to write Ann is your person. Ann is the author of the **Entrepreneurs Guide to Self-Publishing** and runs Post Pre-Press Group found here https://www.postprepress.com.au/

- To **my clients,** who took the time to give me crucial feedback. Your stories are what make me keep doing what I do. Thank you.

- To **my amazing team, past and present, at Life Law Solutions**, who keep everything ticking along, particularly on writing days!
- To my friends **Rachel** and **Jenny**, who support whatever adventure I head off on.
- To **my family** for their support.
- And to **my husband Fraser**. I couldn't have achieved all that I have achieved without you standing beside me, picking me up, keeping me going and supporting me on whatever adventure lies around the corner. Your love and support means so much.

Resources

AUTHOR CONTACT DETAILS

Elizabeth Fairon is a Legal Practice Director at Life Law Solutions. You can contact Elizabeth at either her Brisbane or Sunshine Coast office as follows:

P: 07 3343 9522 or 07 5446 1745

Email: mail@lifelaw.com.au

Web: www.lifelaw.com.au

LinkedIn: @elizabethfairon

★ All website references in this section are current as at 30 June 2023 ★

All types of relationships

You can find information about your local registry of births, deaths and marriages here:

Queensland	https://www.qld.gov.au/law/births-deaths-marriages-and-divorces
New South Wales	http://www.bdm.nsw.gov.au/
Victoria	https://www.bdm.vic.gov.au/
Australian Capital Territory	https://www.accesscanberra.act.gov.au/s/article/apply-for-a-birth-death-or-marriage-certificate-tab-overview
Tasmania	http://www.justice.tas.gov.au/bdm
South Australia	https://www.sa.gov.au/topics/family-and-community/births,-deaths-and-marriages
Northern Territory	https://nt.gov.au/law/bdm
Western Australia	http://www.bdm.dotag.wa.gov.au/

What about the kids?

The reference to the Australian Instituted of Family Studies (AIFS) and the extensive research undertaken by AIFS can be found here:

https://aifs.gov.au/research/family-law

The Journal of Child Psychology and Psychiatry reference can be found here:

https://onlinelibrary.wiley.com/doi/full/10.1111/jcpp.12953

You may need a university or state library subscription to access the article.

The reference to information about general attachment theory and John Bowlby can be found here:

http://www.psychology.sunysb.edu/attachment/online/inge_origins%20DP1992.pdf

Also here: Burton, Lorelle. *Psychology.* 6th ed. Melbourne: Wiley, 2022, pages 784 to 786

Parenting Applications

The following is a list of some of the parenting applications which are available to assist parents in communicating and organising parenting arrangements. There are several parenting applications available from a simple search in your usual search engine. The inclusion of the application in this list shouldn't be taken as an endorsement of that application, simply a list of applications commonly used by families. Families should do significant research to find the right tool including considering where data is stored, how data is tracked, usability and cost.

2Houses: https://www.2houses.com/en/

AppClose: https://appclose.com/

MyMob: https://www.mymob.com/

Our Family Wizard: https://www.ourfamilywizard.com.au/

Parentship: https://play.google.com/store/apps/details?id=com.labs108.teddy&hl=en&gl=US

Talking Parents: https://talkingparents.com/home

We Parent: https://apps.apple.com/us/app/weparent-co-parenting-app/id1441850251

Apples and Oranges

In the section '**Mum and dad will pay for the wedding and other gift stories**' the legal principles about the treatment of gifts of land and money are from two cases:

In the Marriage of Gosper (1987) FLC 91–818

In the Marriage of Kessey (1994) FLC 92-495

The case study about Harry and Isobel's financial agreement is loosely based on the case of *Thorne v Kennedy [2017] HCA 49*

Ready for the future

In each state or territory there is a Public Trustee or Trusts Office where you can obtain further information about the preparation of wills and enduring powers of attorney:

Queensland	https://www.pt.qld.gov.au/
New South Wales	https://www.tag.nsw.gov.au/
Victoria	https://www.statetrustees.com.au/
Australian Capital Territory	https://www.ptg.act.gov.au/
Tasmania	https://www.publictrustee.tas.gov.au/
South Australia	https://www.publictrustee.sa.gov.au/
Northern Territory	https://nt.gov.au/law/processes/about-public-trustee
Western Australia	https://www.wa.gov.au/organisation/ department-of-justice/public-trustee

Empowered by information

You can find more information and resources about the topics covered in this book at lifelaw.com.au.

OTHER KEY AGENCIES

Relationships Australia: https://www.relationships.org.au/ Phone:1300 364 277

Family Relationships: http://www.familyrelationships.gov.au/ Phone: 1800 050 321

Centacare: http://centacarebrisbane.net.au/Phone: 1300 236 822

Anglicare: https://anglicaresq.org.au/children-and-families/family-and-relationship-support/relationship-support/Phone: 1300 610 610

Better Relationships: http://betterrelationships.org.au/services/counselling/Phone: 1300 114 397

Family & Relationship Services Australia Directory: https://frsa.org.au/ Lists centres all throughout Australia.

Legal Aid *services in your State or Territory.*

www.ingramcontent.com/pod-product-compliance
Lightning Source LLC
Chambersburg PA
CBHW072144020426
42334CB00018B/1882